MY FATHER AND I

MY FATHER AND I

by
Camelia
Sadat

Macmillan Publishing Company
New York

Grateful acknowledgment is made for permission to reprint material from
In Search of Identity by Anwar el-Sadat. Copyright © 1977, 1978 by The
Village of Mit Abul-Kum. English translation copyright © 1977, 1978 by
Harper & Row, Publishers, Inc. Reprinted by permission of Harper & Row,
Publishers, Inc.

Macmillan Publishing Company
866 Third Avenue, New York, N.Y. 10022
Collier Macmillan Canada, Inc.

Library of Congress Cataloging-in-Publication Data
Sadat, Camelia.
My father and I.
Includes index.
1. Sadat, Anwar, 1918– .   2. Sadat, Camelia.
3. Egypt—Presidents—Biography.   4. Sadat, Anwar,
1918– —Family—Biography.   I. Title.
DT107.828.S23S22   1985   962'.054'0922 [B]   85-15325
ISBN 0-02-606670-X

Macmillan books are available at special discounts for bulk purchases
for sales promotions, premiums, fund-raising, or educational use.
For details, contact:

Special Sales Director
Macmillan Publishing Company
866 Third Avenue
New York, N.Y. 10022

10 9 8 7 6 5 4 3 2 1

Designed by Jack Meserole

Printed in the United States of America

TO EKBAL

For faith and love. For patience and forgiveness.

TO MY FATHER

The believer. For courage and sacrifice.

Contents

Acknowledgments

I will always be deeply grateful to my publisher and dear friend, Hillel Black, who believed not only in my book but also in me. His inspiration, suggestions, and support are the things that guided and helped my book and me. I thank him for giving me a chance.

I am in debt to my dearest friend and collaborator, Dr. Robert E. Simmons. Before working with me on this book, Dr. Simmons was my professor for two years, fascinating me by his great knowledge of other cultures and his constant desire to learn more every day. Working with him on the book, I have learned what discipline, dedication, and accomplishment are. When I was most frustrated and when I needed help most he was my great supporter. I will always appreciate the valuable knowledge, advice, and time that he gave me and the pleasure I derived from working with him. I look forward to working with him again, for I am still the student who learned a little from her great professor.

I give my special thanks to my editor, Rosemary Ford, an intelligent and talented young woman who through her eagerness for good work provoked many beautiful memories and added a valuable touch to my book. I've learned a lot from her thinking "in a loud voice."

I am grateful to Ambassador Tahseen M. Basheer, who kindly gave of his invaluable time and expertise when the book was written.

I am indebted to my attorney, adviser, and great friend Bob Woolf of Boston for his wonderful enthusiasm and professional advice whenever I needed it. Thank you my dear friend.

I am also grateful to all those who were involved in the production of the book for their fine work and to all my friends who unfailingly encouraged and supported me.

Finally, my heartfelt thanks to my daughter, Lulee, for her sweet forbearance, understanding, and support while I was involved in this book, especially during those times when I had to be away from her.

Preface

It used to be that when a family member died away from home the news would be delivered by a personal phone call, in somber but sympathetic tones, or by someone who rang the doorbell and stood there uneasily trying to decide how to break the news.

However, in this age of mass communication, I first learned of my father's death on October 6, 1981, from CBS-TV anchorman Dan Rather as I sat before my television set in my living room in Boston. Dan Rather heard of Father's death at almost the same instant, talking via satellite to a newswoman who was half a world away in Cairo, Egypt. As I listened, millions of others around the globe received the news along with me.

My father's death was given this attention because he was the president of Egypt and had been assassinated by Islamic fanatics. They attacked him as he and other officials reviewed a major military procession in Nasser City, outside Cairo. His murderers contended that they were justified because my father was a traitor to his people. His alleged treachery was that he had gone to Jerusalem in search of peace between Arabs and Israelis and had subsequently co-signed the Camp David peace accords with Israeli Prime Minister Menachem Begin. My father's name was Anwar el-Sadat.

My name is Camelia Sadat. I am the third daughter of the slain Egyptian leader.

I had been living in the United States for about two months, but because I was using an assumed name for security reasons only a few confidants knew I was a Sadat. It was feared that if people learned and revealed my identity, I myself might become a target for Middle Eastern fanatics.

Now, several years after my father's death and my decision to use my family name while I am in the United States, people are often confused about my family. "I respected your father very much," they tell me. I am grateful for their recognition of my father. They then continue, "I also admire your mother, Jihan, very much." I agree that Jihan is admirable. I love her and have great respect for her. However, Father's second wife, Jihan, is not my mother. My mother is Ekbal Mohammed Madi, the divorced first wife of Anwar el-Sadat.

My father divorced my mother the year I was born. She never remarried. My father, a devout Muslim, loved and supported his three daughters by his first wife—Rokaya, Rawia, and me.

That most people never suspected that my father had had another wife at an earlier time is part of the story I will tell here. My account deals with the original family of Anwar el-Sadat, which is virtually unknown to the people of Egypt or to the world.

When I left Egypt to study in the United States, I had decided that the only way to search for my own identity would be to leave both Father and my country. In this way, I thought, I would be able to sort out my life, given enough time.

During his lifetime, I was unable to talk at length with my father about my problems. It was difficult for me to express my feelings toward him, because both my parents had taught me from birth to believe in the Koran. There, in *Surat Bani-Isra-il*, it is written:

> Thy Lord hath decreed
> That ye worship none but Him,
> And that ye be kind
> To parents. Whether one
> Or both of them attain
> Old age in thy life,
> Say not to them a word
> Of contempt, nor repel them,
> But address them
> In terms of honor.
>
> And, out of kindness,
> Lower to them the wing
> Of humility, and say:
> "My Lord! bestow on them
> Thy mercy even as they
> Cherished me in childhood."

Consequently, for me to challenge my father would have been an exceptional act of disobedience.

Twice, I considered defying my background. I thought I would write my father a personal letter that would reveal my thoughts as well as my love for him. But I could not bring myself to do this during his lifetime. Early in my adult life I feared his wrath. Later, I feared that I might hurt or offend him to the point that instead of understanding me, he might reject me.

I lost my chance to the three bullets of the assassins that struck Father's body. But what I will present in the following pages is what I should have tried to tell him.

As someone who firmly believes in her Muslim religion and a spiritual afterlife, I have reason to hope that my father will yet hear my thoughts and will understand and forgive a daughter's need to speak her heart.

Boston, 1985

MY FATHER AND I

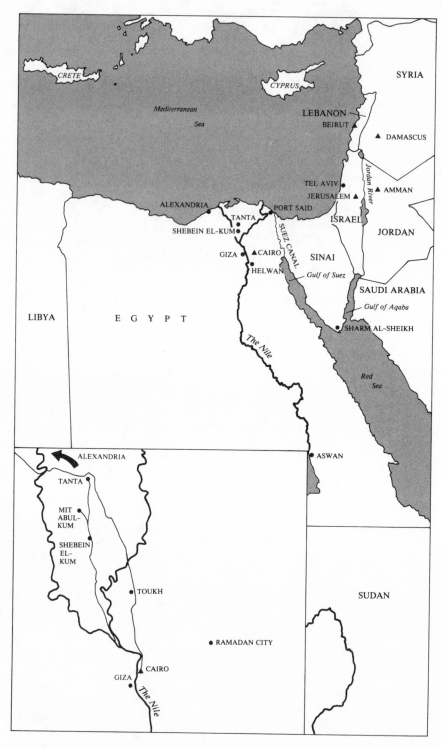

Egypt and Environs with Inset of the Nile Delta

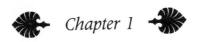 *Chapter 1*

MIT ABUL-KUM

MY FAMILY'S VILLAGE is Mit Abul-Kum. It is located in the verdant Nile Delta of Egypt, about seventy miles from Cairo. Now it is the center for a thriving agricultural community of four thousand people. On its outskirts are fields that yield cotton, corn, and fruit.

In the 1920s it was one of many villages in Egypt, with a small population of fifteen hundred. People lived as they had lived for thousands of years. When the crops failed or the rain did not fall they would shrug and immediately begin working in the fields for next year, accepting that this year there would be no festival for the harvest and less money for food and clothing.

The only contact between Mit Abul-Kum and the outside world was through travelers, Gypsies, and visiting government officials, particularly the mailman. Twice a year, many villagers would make their way to Tanta, the closest big town, to buy new clothes for the religious feast days. It was a major event, and families would ride the twelve miles to Tanta on donkeys. However, Cairo and Alexandria might well have been foreign nations to them. There were no radios and no electricity. The village was a world unto itself.

Families would grow their own vegetables, and when they needed additional food they would buy it directly from the fields. They also raised their own livestock. Their cows provided milk, and cheese and bread, staples of the diet, were made at home. One of the few entrepreneurs in the village was a woman who sold candles from a tent beside a main street. In the morning, the tent would appear like some exotic blossom. At night, like a day-blooming flower, it would disappear.

At sunrise each workday the men who labored in the fields went to work, usually in groups. The wives stayed at home in the morning to milk the cows, bake bread, make cheese, and prepare noon meals for their husbands. At midday they walked to the fields with their

1

lunch containers to eat with their husbands. Then they remained to work the afternoon away with the men, until it was time to go home.

Mit Abul-Kum is still a place made for children accustomed to simple pleasures. There are huge mulberry and fig trees to climb. In those days, during the parching heat of the summer a truck from the district government came to sprinkle water on the dusty, unpaved streets—an occasion for daring boys to run after the truck, the hems of their short, dresslike galabias held between clenched teeth to free their flashing legs for the chase. The village children also relished the prospect of taking a refreshing swim in a nearby lake formed when a government project opened the Nile River from Cairo to Alexandria.

One summer day in the mid-1920s, when the heat had risen to between 100 and 110 degrees Fahrenheit, a group of children headed toward the lake. Two of them were named Salem and Said. They were sons of the mayor of Mit Abul-Kum, Mohammed Madi. Tagging along was a dark-skinned younger boy named Anwar, a frequent companion of the Madi boys.

"Come on, Anwar," the others teased. "Do you want to cool off or not?" Anwar, the youngest, hurried along, eager to prove himself the equal of the older children.

At the water's edge the Madi boys jumped and disappeared under the murky brown water before popping up like corks. Anwar, too, jumped into the lake. But, unlike them, he went under and came up in a panic. He did not know how to swim. As he opened his mouth to scream, water rushed in and partly strangled his cry. Salem Madi became aware of Anwar's plight and quickly stroked toward him as he disappeared again. Salem grasped Anwar and pulled him to the shore.

I have heard this story again and again from Salem and Said since my own childhood. Salem and Said Madi were destined to become the brothers-in-law of the rescued Anwar, their childhood playmate. And this incident became an often-told story in the Madi family. For if it had not been for the quick action of Salem that day, there would have been no Egyptian President Anwar el-Sadat and no internationally recognized statesman or Nobel Prize–winning peacemaker.

Anwar el-Sadat was the son of Mohammed el-Sadat, a military clerk. His father appeared infrequently in Mit Abul-Kum during Anwar's youth because he was often detained by army service in the Sudan, then part of Anglo Egypt. The village knew Anwar's mother as Sit el-Barein, literally "the Lady of the Two Sides," reflecting her half-Egyptian and half-Sudanese lineage. She was a short woman with deep coffee-colored skin. She usually dressed in black. A *tarha* (head cover) concealed her hair, as custom prescribes. It is believed that the hair and other parts of a woman's body should be covered in order not to tempt men. Her garments were long-sleeved to conceal her arms, and the hem of her full skirt reached the floor.

Anwar's family lived in the mud-walled home of his grandmother Om Mohammed ("Mother of Mohammed"). Among villagers and members of the middle class, a wife whose firstborn is a son changes her name to "mother of" that son. If the first child is a daughter, however, the woman retains her own name. Om Mohammed's house had one big room for living. Each corner contained a mattress—one for Sit el-Barein and her children, one for Mohammed el-Sadat when he returned to the village, one for Om Mohammed, and one for Mohammed's other wife, Amina, and her children.

During the course of his life Mohammed el-Sadat had eight wives. The first six bore him no children, so he divorced them one after the other. Sit el-Barein, his seventh wife, bore him four children—Talaat, Anwar, Esmat, and a daughter, Nafeisa. When Mohammed el-Sadat decided to take an eighth wife he did not divorce Sit el-Barein, because under Islamic rules a man is entitled to more than one wife. Amina, his eighth wife, bore him nine children during their marriage. Sit el-Barein and Amina were both natives of Mit Abul-Kum.

Islamic rules allow men to have as many as four wives simultaneously. A man can marry a woman of any religion, since the children are always raised in the father's religion, thus spreading the faith. But the rule also ensures that the women always have a protector and provider. For a man who wants a second wife is required to guarantee that he can provide equal lodging for both wives. In addition, he must equalize his financial and emotional support for each wife. The husband's failure to treat each wife equally this way constitutes grounds for the offended one to petition for divorce.

This is not to say that women have to marry. Even in those days, in Egyptian villages a single woman might go to some respected male in the community and enlist him to take care of her property and hire men to work her land. When it was time for the harvest, her appointed male representative would deal with buyers and receive some commission for his efforts.

After she lost her husband Om Mohammed did not commission anyone to help with the farm business. She was a very independent woman, and she did not want to lose a piaster from the earnings of her land. She herself hired men to work for her, although that was unusual. She was a tough boss, according to all accounts. She swore a lot, and her voice "was heard all over the village." She also drank coffee and smoked cigarettes at a time when both were considered exclusively male habits. Her behavior made her something of an outcast in the village.

No one escaped Om Mohammed's tongue-lashings, least of all her daughters-in-law, Sit el-Barein and Amina. Sit el-Barein was a particular target of Om Mohammed's wrath. Om Mohammed had Turkish lineage, and her son, Mohammed, had blue eyes, blond hair, and fair skin. Om Mohammed hated the dark-skinned Sit el-Barein, for her own mother as well as her sisters and brothers had lighter complexions. Anwar inherited Sit el-Barein's coloring.

Om Mohammed forced her own son to get an education, and she insisted on the same for her grandchildren. Young Anwar was sent to El Kottab, a school that was conducted by a religious leader. It was the only formal school in Mit Abul-Kum, and it was for boys only. Girls received their education at home, under the tutelage of some educated family member.

At El Kottab, Anwar learned to read and write, and in order to graduate the students had to commit the Koran to memory. All his life he was to be deeply religious, praying so often that he developed the "prayer knot" of devout Muslims, a permanent callus on the forehead that comes from touching the prayer mat repeatedly. Later, Om Mohammed would arrange to send my father and his brother Talaat to a Coptic Christian school in the village of Toukh, about half a mile from Mit Abul-Kum.

At night Om Mohammed would tell bedtime stories to Anwar

and his brothers and sisters. In an autobiography published near the end of his life, *In Search of Identity*, my father recalled how Om Mohammed's storytelling, which often focused on themes of courage and daring, contributed to his political consciousness.

One of these stories dealt with the poisoning of Mustafa Kamil—one of our political leaders—by the British, who wanted to put an end to his struggle against their occupation of Egypt. I did not know at the time who Mustafa Kamil was or that he actually died in his prime. I knew only, at that tender age, that there were forces, called "the British," who were alien to us, and that they were evil because they poisoned people.

His book speaks of another tale that left a lifelong impression on him. It was based on an actual incident. British soldiers were shooting pigeons when a stray bullet set a wheat silo on fire. When farmers gathered because of the fire, one of the soldiers fired a shot at them. The Egyptians pursued him and a fight resulted in which a British soldier was killed. The foreigners arrested many Egyptians and held a court-martial. Before the sentences were announced, they built gallows. Some of the Egyptians who had been arrested were hanged; others were whipped. But an Egyptian named Zahran became the hero of the incident because he fought valiantly and was defiant unto death. He had stood up to the aggressors and protected the honor of his people.

The village itself was also a lasting model for my father. The agrarian life of the village stressed the interdependence of members of the community. Without the aid and psychological support of friends and neighbors, survival for a family would be difficult. The coming together of community members for work and for special observances such as weddings and funerals constituted a continuing affirmation of that interdependence. That mutual reliance and strength of village life became a theme in Anwar's later political speeches, in which he often referred to Egypt as a large village. And as president, he would hear complaints from the students at Cairo University with the patience, skill, and humor of a village *omda*, or mayor.

Salem and Said's father was Mohammed Madi, the *omda* of Mit Abul-Kum. Villagers recognized Madi as one of the relatively affluent persons in their community. The Madi family lived in one of the only two homes in the village made of concrete rather than mud, which was a serviceable building material in view of the limited rainfall in the area.

Mit Abul-Kum's center of activity was El Dawar, a centrally located meetinghouse that was run by the *omda*. As one of the wealthiest persons in the village, Mohammed Madi had the responsibility of providing assistance and hospitality for villagers and visitors at El Dawar. Because of the need for wealth, the *omda's* job would be inherited. Nearly every day he could be seen sitting outside the building, listening to the complaints and petitions of the villagers. As for visitors, El Dawar had sleeping facilities for travelers who wished to spend the night.

Anwar was no stranger to the Madi household. He often went there to play with the Madi boys and with their sister Ekbal. Their mother, Rokaya, readily included a place setting at her *tableia*—a traditional round dining table that is nine inches above the floor— for young Anwar. Rokaya was well known and respected in the village. She not only managed her household but became increasingly involved in the financial management of her family's farming activities after her husband died.

Ekbal Madi was a very quiet girl. Her mother trained her to cook, sew, and take care of the house—much like most Egyptian girls of her generation. One of her uncles taught her to read and write. She also learned to make herbal medicines. To this day, villagers still approach Ekbal asking for her famous eye drops. "Nothing like them," they tell her.

Ekbal was also a little mother to her four brothers and two half brothers. After her father died, and her mother became involved with running the business, she helped raise the children. "After I am gone," her mother warned her, "you will be the one who keeps them together. You must listen to their problems," Mother Rokaya said. "Pay attention to their differences. Do not think so much of yourself. Remember who we are and who you are."

Ekbal was taught to hope for a good husband and a family. That was as much as any young woman should expect, she was told. Getting a good husband was the aspiration of every village girl, and still is. If the husband was not rich, that was not important, as long as he was a good man and came from a good family. By working side by side a couple could always build wealth, the elders said.

Ekbal was six years old when her father died. Until she married, she had never traveled farther from the village than Tanta, where the family bought clothes. Only after she was married would she go to Cairo for the first time, to select furniture for her house. Mother Rokaya was concerned with family dignity on that Cairo trip. "Stop gawking," she ordered Ekbal. "Do not look like a stupid person who knows nothing. This is just like Tanta, only bigger."

In 1925, when Anwar was seven years old, his father returned from military service in the Sudan. The British high commissioner for the Sudan, Sir Lee Stack, had been assassinated in Cairo the previous year. One of the sanctions the British imposed in retaliation was that the Egyptian army would be withdrawn from the Sudan.

Young Anwar was taken to Cairo, along with his mother and her other children, and Amina and her children. There he would continue his education. Though the family home in Mit Abul-Kum was sold, Anwar was allowed to return to the village to visit for four months each summer. The Madi family invited him to spend most of that time in their home.

Until she reached the age of ten there was routine contact between Ekbal and Anwar. Then their relationship changed. It was not deemed appropriate for young men and women to mix. Ekbal's brothers and half brothers would take their meal at one time, Ekbal at another. The boys lived in one area of the house, a shallow but lengthy building, and Ekbal in another. However, the custom of the house did not discourage the budding romance. Young Ekbal would station herself at her window, and Anwar seemed to sense that she was not there only to "take the air."

One of Ekbal's brothers became upset. "It is not proper for Ekbal to be carrying on with Anwar through the window," he protested to Mother Rokaya. But love blossomed at that window like the fragrant jasmine that grew under it.

In 1940, when Anwar was twenty-two and Ekbal twenty-three, he asked for her hand in marriage. Her half brother Mohammed was then the mayor of Mit Abul-Kum. Anwar had joined the Egyptian army two years earlier. He had completed high school in Cairo.

He also had been graduated from the Royal Military Academy. The experience had turned him into a dashing young soldier determined to liberate his country from its British oppressors.

He would always be an insatiable reader, and during this period he read about revolutions, about those who burned to liberate their country from colonialism. His earlier experience demonstrating against British rule while he was in high school had also developed his political consciousness. He still dreamed of Zahran. "I hoped my [own] story would grow into a ballad that would live in the hearts of posterity," he would write in *In Search of Identity*.

Anwar's Muslim culture dictated that he was at a point in life when he should get married. For a Muslim male, marriage is half of the religion. Anwar had followed his faith with dedication since he attended El Kottab, praying five times a day, fasting during Ramadan, an annual period of fasting and prayer, reciting the Muslim testimony every day ("There is no God except for Allah, and Mohammed is the messenger of Allah . . ."), and contributing to charities. He had not yet made the pilgrimage to the house of God in Mecca, but he was ready to accept the responsibilities of marriage. He needed a wife to guarantee a home life for him, enabling him to meet his life's obligations.

The marriage proposal did not go over well with Ekbal's half brother Mohammed. Neither did it please Abbas, her other half brother. A perceived difference in social status was the bone of contention. "Who does this Anwar think he is anyhow?" was the attitude.

Ekbal's father had been the mayor of Mit Abul-Kum, he had a large home, and his family was involved in farming. But more than that, he had held the honorary title of bey. At that time, it was customary for the government to bestow the title of pasha or bey as distinctions. Such titles were given to heads of communities who assumed responsibility for their people. In fact, Ekbal's father had been given his honorary title after making a gift of a beautiful horse to a high government official, Khedive Abbas Helmy II, when he visited the village. "Anwar—what does he have? Only his uniform," snorted one of Ekbal's brothers incredulously. Ekbal's brothers Salem and Said sided with their sister and their former playmate Anwar. Ekbal, they knew, loved her young suitor.

Ekbal was ready for marriage. Her mother had been training her to be the head of a household since she was twelve. But despite her household obligations, Ekbal had relatively little to do socially. Much time was spent playing with her niece. She also occupied herself with decorative needlework.

Ekbal was a comely woman by this time. At five feet one, she was shorter than her suitor, who was five feet ten inches tall. Her eyes are a deep brown—so dark, in fact, that even close up they appear black. A photo of her at this time shows her with glossy black hair. She usually wore it straight. Her face, with its fine porcelain skin, was oval. It framed a small, finely drawn mouth.

Mother Rokaya would not hear of any argument against Anwar's appropriateness as a suitor based on his lack of affluence. "To God," she said, "we are all poor and all his servants." She called Ekbal aside. "Do you like him, child?" she inquired, watching Ekbal's eyes.

There was no coy hesitation in the response. "Yes, Mother, I like him. I want to marry him."

"Well," said Mother Rokaya, "I like him a lot, too." Turning to the young men of her family, she declared, "I am her mother, and I say yes." Teasing, she declared to Mohammed and Abbas, "Since you are Ekbal's half brothers, you do not get full votes."

So it was that my parents, Ekbal Mohammed Madi and her young soldier suitor, Anwar el-Sadat, came to be married.

In one respect my mother's half brothers were right about the impending marriage—Anwar el-Sadat was financially hard-up. Yet, somehow, he scrambled around until he came up with the money for two wedding bands. That was in the summer of 1940, and members of both families occupied themselves with preparations for the marriage.

In the home of Mohammed el-Sadat in Cairo, the family readied a room to receive Anwar and Ekbal after their marriage ceremony. Ekbal's family was buying a bedroom suite and preparing a trousseau for the bride. Due to the local prominence of the Madi family, the wedding was to be something of an event in the village.

•

When the time for the wedding came it was November 1940, and the days were fair and somewhat cooler in the village. Everyone in the family concentrated on last-minute preparations, for there would be a three-day celebration. Mother's memories helped me reconstruct what happened.

The night before the signing of the wedding contract friends held a henna party, something like a shower and bachelor party combined. Both the bride and the bridegroom attend, but the bridegroom is the only male. The name "henna party" comes from a traditional use of the coloring agent henna, which has either red or white flowers and blossoms that have the fragrance of roses. The extract from the plant's leaves is used as a dye, and it has a reddish-brown color. During the henna party the dye is mixed with water and usually applied to color the hands and feet of both the bride and the bridegroom. It is considered a kind of blessing for the couple and helps to perpetuate the memory of that festive night.

It is a Muslim belief that God takes to heaven those who die as virgins. At a wedding, the henna is used to "mark" the bridal couple and all those who attend as a blessing of that spiritual purity. In this henna party, the celebrants applied just a small dot of henna coloring, but the giggles and smiles made it clear that no matter how little or how much the henna, there were fervent wishes for the new couple's happiness and well-being.

As was customary, too, all of the women at the henna party danced for the bridegroom. Anwar was properly attentive. As though mesmerized by the hypnotic music, his eyes followed the graceful moves of the dancers as they turned slowly. Much of the music was accompanied by soul-stirring popular or traditional lyrics that dwelt on love's encounters. Anwar's smile flashed as he became caught up in the festive goings-on. His gaze fell often upon Ekbal's attractive face. She returned his attention. My man, she thought. He is handsome. He will be a good husband.

As was the tradition, each of the three days, my mother's family slaughtered an animal. It was part of the ceremony of blessing. The first portion was given to the poor of the village; the rest went to the family. The fact that the family was able to conduct a fresh slaughter each day and share its largesse was not only a celebration of the wedding but a reminder to the community of my mother's affluence.

Relatives and friends also sent food and other gifts for the couple. Money and jewelry arrived. There were ducks and pigeons, which are considered delicacies, especially in the country. When foodstuffs were sent, the giver demonstrated his own wealth by sending several of each item.

On the first day the wedding contract was signed, Anwar's mother, father, stepmother, grandmother, and elder brother, Talaat, were there to represent their side. That night was the wedding night. No more romancing through the window, Anwar thought, looking at his bride. Now we are man and wife.

On the second day, my mother was up early to prepare food for her husband. According to tradition, she would cook to please her man only. The other women of the household would cook for everyone else. Egyptian villagers truly enjoy their food. The basic diet consists of three staples—vegetables, rice, and meat. The rice and meat are used to stuff various types of vegetables, such as potatoes, zucchini, tomatoes, eggplant, and bell peppers, while others are cooked with tomato sauce and meat. The meat is usually lamb, chunks of which are cooked like shish kebab.

Each dish takes on a different flavor depending upon how garlic and onion are combined with various sauces. Cooked pigeons and rabbits have always been considered delicacies. Even now my mother carefully tends rabbits and pigeons on the roof of her Cairo apartment building in order to embellish her table with these treats. For dessert there were rich plates of baklava made of layers of filo dough, crushed nuts, and honey. And there was *konafa*, a shredded dough fried in butter and mixed with different kinds of nuts.

In the country people usually eat with their hands, but Mother Rokaya had a silver set and her children were brought up differently. On my visits to the village, relatives who are accustomed to eating with their hands courteously attempt to cope with spoons and forks, everyone competing to prove he can master the technique. Anyone who has observed Americans or Europeans trying to eat with chopsticks will appreciate the difficulty of the transition and the occasionally funny experiences that result.

That day Mother Rokaya had rented tables and chairs to accommodate the crowd of family and guests. My father was the only man at his table. The other men of the family were having the same dinner, but they were being served at El Dawar. Both the men and the women wore long galabias, known to Westerners as caftans. They are dresslike garments well suited to Egypt's climate. During the hot months the loose galabia affords a cool flow of air. In winter the same garment wraps the body to keep it warm. The main difference between the galabias worn by men and those worn by women is the coloring and decoration. Men tend to wear solid colors, particularly black and white. Women use all colors but prefer brighter hues and often have the garments decorated with elaborate designs. At their wedding, my father proudly wore his army uniform and my mother had a white wedding gown.

The ceremony drew family and people from Mit Abul-Kum, as well as other nearby villages, who considered it an obligation to share major events such as weddings or funerals with those whom they cherish and respect. Usually the celebration begins by noon and ends at about sundown. This one ended at about 4:30 P.M. because the month was November and sundown came early. There was an obligation to entertain, but talking was the main activity. When the men in the family had to leave to tend business in the fields they worked quickly and rushed back to the house to share in talk, jokes, and gossip.

The third day of the wedding festivities repeated the pattern of the second day. Much of the talk reconsidered family history, re-hashed interesting things that had transpired in the village or affected individual members of the community, or speculated on current events. Their talk was an affirmation of the bonds that held everyone together. Actually, the wedding seemed to go on and on, because Anwar and Ekbal spent the next week in Mother Rokaya's home in Mit Abul-Kum.

When the time came for the young couple to leave for Cairo, they embraced the family. Neither of them would live permanently in Mit Abul-Kum again. But the spirit of this village would never leave them. Throughout the rest of his life, my father would often return to the village and some of his most important political decisions were made there. As he later wrote in *In Search of Identity*:

Wherever I go, wherever I happen to be, I shall always know . . . that I have living roots there, deep down in the soil of my village, in that land out of which I grew, like the trees and the plants.

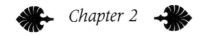

Chapter 2

EKBAL AND ANWAR

ANWAR took Ekbal to live in his father's home, a big house in a Cairo suburb. The entrance opened onto a large central hallway. There were two spacious bedrooms on the left and two more on the right. The back bedroom on the right awaited the newlyweds. At the end of the hall a stairway led down to the kitchen.

Soon after her arrival in the household my mother encountered friction born of envy. Since her father was a bey, she was rightfully addressed as *Hanem* (Lady) Ekbal. Anwar's mother, Sit el-Barein, who was fond of her new daughter-in-law, addressed her by that title. That did not sit well at all with Mohammed el-Sadat's wife Amina nor with the wife of his son Talaat, who had married after the family's move to Cairo. The mere sound of the words "Hanem Ekbal" was grounds for dispute. Amina and Talaat's wife insulted Ekbal and Sit el-Barein defended her vigorously. They felt offended that my mother had brought a servant from the village. And, perhaps worse, my mother stayed out of these fights, which was even greater provocation.

There were ripples from the conflict. Sit el-Barein, who was in effect the head woman of the household, was punished by her husband because she could not control the conduct of his other wife Amina. For a time, he banned Sit el-Barein from his presence during lunches. No one said life would be without its turbulence.

My mother said that in the winter of 1941, when she was twenty-four years old, she began to observe that Father entertained strangers at the house. She was not expected to act as hostess. The strangers, it turned out, were members of the Muslim Brotherhood, an organization that strongly believed that the corruption of Egypt's King Farouk should be eliminated by imposing Islamic rule on the country.

King Farouk was the last ruling descendant of Mohammed Ali.

His family had ruled Egypt since the 1800s. The British, who came to Egypt at the beginning of the nineteenth century and who wanted to protect their colonial interests against the French and other European powers, supported Farouk. Six decades earlier, in 1882, the British had intervened militarily in Egypt to protect the royal government against an active political threat. The British presence remained in Egypt until 1956.

Although World War II was well under way at this time, Egypt's involvement was marginal. The British were in Egypt, but they wanted to use Egypt as a safe base during the war and did not want to involve Egypt in their battle against the Axis powers. Egypt eventually joined the war at its end so that it could become a member of the United Nations. At one point the British and German General Rommel's panzer tank forces fought in Egypt's western deserts, about three hundred miles from Cairo. However, certain nationalist factions in Egypt thought the Germans might be used as leverage to oust the British overlords from Egypt. Others, like those who were visiting my father, were concerned with first getting rid of Farouk. The men met alone. Afterward, Mother went into the room where the meeting had occurred and found her husband hiding books and papers. "Something from my work . . . nothing important," he told her.

In summer, pregnant with her first child, Ekbal returned to Mit Abul-Kum. It was customary for an expectant woman to be with her family at the child's birth, permitting them to take care of the mother. Sit el-Barein accompanied her daughter-in-law to the village for the summer. It was a tranquil time for both of them, especially after the conflicts in the Cairo household. On September 6, 1941, the Sadats' first child, a daughter, was born. She was named Rokaya, for Ekbal's mother.

Anwar came to the village to visit his wife only after Rokaya was born. He had been moved to a military base outside Cairo that was very far from Mit Abul-Kum, and travel was difficult in those days. No one in the family had an auto, so the journey involved a train trip to Tanta, the largest city in the state where the village was located, then a ride in a collective—an old car with a driver—which transported passengers to the villages.

Mother said that when it was time for her to return to Cairo, her family plied her with a little of this and a little of that until it seemed there was enough wheat, butter, coffee, sugar, and other food to provision the Cairo household for an entire year. When I last visited Cairo my mother insisted on cramming my bags full of her special coffee, spices, herbs and herbal remedies for cramps and headaches, rice and *doq-qa*. *Doq-qa* is a high-protein powder flavored with salt, which travelers use on their long treks across the desert, and my mother obviously fears that survival in the United States is as difficult as on those desert journeys. "Watch out for the bad road and the deep sea," she will always say in parting, echoing her own mother's words.

My father brought mother, the baby Rokaya, and his own mother back to Cairo. Shortly afterward, he began to have trouble with the police. It began rather quietly. Following Father's return to Cairo with his family, the police came to the door asking for Anwar el-Sadat. "He is at the military base," they were told.

On the second day my father informed his family that he had been arrested. He was a suspect in the case of an Egyptian opposition leader, Aziz al-Masri, who was wanted by the government for his work in the liberation movement. The politician had tried to flee the country.

The friends of Aziz al-Masri had obtained a plane for his escape from Egypt, but, incredibly, no one remembered to obtain fuel for the flight. The government began to hunt down those who were suspected of aiding the attempted escape. My father was cleared and released the same day. However, his troubles with the authorities were just beginning.

Father was soon approached by German agents in Cairo. They wanted to give him a shortwave radio transmitter and have him send information to aid the Axis forces. Father saw this as a way to strike back at the British. It would mean help for the Germans who were harassing the British Eighth Army. My father reasoned that if the British were defeated, the Axis powers would help kick the British out of Egypt. He lugged the radio home. The German agents evidently possessed as much skill as the Keystone Kops, for soon they were in the custody of the authorities, and fingers were pointed at the twenty-three-year-old Anwar el-Sadat.

At 3:00 A.M. one morning in 1942 Mother told me that she

heard voices at the front of the house. She was in bed with Father. Then someone began to bang on the door, yelling something about the police. "Anwar! Anwar!" mother cried, shaking her sleeping husband. "There is someone calling for you. Wake up!"

When Father went to the door it became obvious that the police's call had something to do with the Germans' spy radio. Members of the family rushed to hide it. They carried the radio to the kitchen and buried it in an old, unused oven under the corncobs used to fuel the cooking fire. The police took Father away.

According to Mother, the next day she pulled the radio from under the pile of corncobs and smashed it into small pieces with a large kitchen pestle. Then she had a family servant, Abdou, take the pulverized spy radio and spread it on a railway track where no one was likely to see it again.

The case against my father fizzled. The authorities were unable to prove he was linked with the Germans. However, under martial law the police held Father as a suspect. But it was enough that he had been implicated in the escape of Aziz al-Masri. There was no court review. Father remained a prisoner from the winter of 1942 until 1945. Being imprisoned was one blow, but a worse one for the family was the news that Father was being dismissed by a military court-martial from the Egyptian army, without pay. What would become of his young family? Without Father's salary Mother and their daughter, Rokaya, would become a burden to his own father.

Father was first held in the Aliens' Jail, in Cairo. Then he was moved about 96 miles away to the Maqusah Jail in the governorate of Menia. A detention center for political prisoners, the jail actually consisted of a small villa that had been taken over from an influential local man. The jail was considered rather posh, because each political prisoner had his own room. It was something like being under house arrest. Prisoners could listen to the radio, read, plant things in the garden, and tend their personal crops. They could even raise rabbits.

Contact with outsiders was another matter, though. A prisoner could receive visits from members of his family only. Mother said that she made monthly visits to her husband, beginning in the summer of 1943 through October 1944. Without the income from Father's army position, Mother had trouble making ends meet. There was no money for travel. Nor was there any money for food to take to her husband, who loved her stuffed pigeons. Consequently, Mother began to sell her jewelry in order to be with Father and offer him whatever comfort she could. When she went she usually carried enough food for a small army. It was a wonder that Father did not take on the proportions of the immense King Farouk.

Often when Mother traveled to Maqusah Jail she went in the company of two women whose brother was also being detained. She dressed fashionably, wearing a Turkish veil. Called a *yashmak*, the veil was associated with aristocratic families. It covered the face from below the eyes and draped to the chest, and was fashioned from fine cloth like satin or silk. Women wore the veil along with a *tarha*. Mother later gave up the veil and *tarha*, and, reflecting her Turkish extraction, began to wear a turban to conceal her hair. It amused Mother to learn that while visiting Father it was once rumored that she was a princess traveling first class with her two chamber ladies. The three women would stay either in a hotel convenient to the jail or with friends. They were allowed to see their relatives in the jail only during the day. Mother told me she looked forward to the trips not only because she could visit Father but also because the travel took her away from the conflict and stress of the Mohammed el-Sadat household.

During this period Mother suffered from both a personal crisis and the attitude of her father-in-law. Her own beloved mother, Rokaya, died in the same month Father was imprisoned. Then her father-in-law began to needle her about his son. "A revolutionary— or a criminal?" he would say. "What is the difference?" A career army man himself, Mohammed el-Sadat placed a high value on loyalty to the government. He could not understand why his son should be such a nettle to the Farouk regime.

Although Sit el-Barein continued to be supportive of my mother, Father's absence from the household combined with Mohammed el-Sadat's animosity was painful for both my mother and Rokaya. The child had been with her father so infrequently because of his imprisonment that she would look at Mohammed el-Sadat and ask, "Is this my father?" Ekbal would respond softly, "No, child, that is your grandfather. Your father is away. But he will return to us soon." At such times Rokaya became upset, and, Mother told me, it was difficult to calm her. Later, when Mother returned from visiting Father she began to bring Rokaya presents, telling her they were sent by her father. That made Rokaya happy—but only briefly. Later, after she had visited Father in the prison yard, Rokaya told people that her father was being held prisoner in a chicken coop.

Mother also suffered when her father-in-law returned home with candy for his young children but not for his granddaughter. He would call his children into his room and give them the treats as though Rokaya should not know. Then, as children will do, the youngsters came out to taunt Rokaya. In many ways Mohammed el-Sadat was unusually hard and insensitive to his son's family. Because of the admonition of the Koran to honor parents and elders, my mother could not bring herself to condemn his behavior, however.

My mother always worried about being a burden to Mohammed el-Sadat, especially after Father lost his army position and his income. But after the government transferred Father to the Maqusah Jail a fellow officer visited him at the Menia Hospital, where he was recovering from an ailment, with news that the Muslim Brotherhood had pledged ten Egyptian pounds a month to support his family in Cairo. At that time a piaster (a hundredth of an Egyptian pound) could buy food for an adequate meal, so the pledge was hardly stingy.

In the winter of 1943 Father was moved to a jail in El Zaytun, a Cairo suburb. Fortunately this would place him closer to his family. Unfortunately, though, the chief of the prison was verbally abusive and unpredictable. Father staged an escape with another prisoner to protest the treatment in the jail. Ekbal's brother Said helped him to escape. He went with his colleague to the palace and demanded an audience.

"This is sheer lunacy," one official said, astounded by Father's audacity. "What in the world must be in your head that you come here, of all places?"

Father was insistent about lodging his protest. It would result in the dismissal of the prison chief. The victory was short-lived, however. The chief had an influential relative in the government who would soon get his kinsman reinstated.

Recalling the escape, Mother told me that on that day she had busied herself with work in her father-in-law's home. Suddenly she looked up and gasped. There, standing before her, was her husband. He had entered very quietly. "I am back for just a little while," he told her. "I want a bath and clean clothes. You have no idea how conditions are in that place."

Father had promised the authorities that he would surrender himself at the jail on the next day. That night, though, he stayed with Mother. Nine months later, a second daughter, who would be named Rawia, issued from that night with his wife.

During 1943 to 1944 it became clear that Germany was on its way to defeat. Father decided that since he had been imprisoned on suspicion of helping the Germans, their impending defeat would render the case against him moot—definitely not worth arguing. He felt that this constituted grounds for reconsideration of not only the case against him but also the one against his friend Hassan Izzat, an army pilot who had introduced him to the German spies. Izzat had been a good friend and companion, helping him to pass the long days in jail.

With the aid of Mother's brother Said, Father and Izzat managed to escape once more from the El Zaytun jail. As he had done at Father's previous escape, Said drove a car to the jail and abandoned it with the engine running for the two fugitives. There seemed to be no real future in going to the authorities to plead his case, so this time Father traveled to another area of Egypt, grew a beard to disguise himself, and took a job loading alabaster from the Pyramids. The truck with which he worked belonged to Izzat. My mother moved to El Zaytun to be with her husband.

From October 1944 to September 1945, Father worked and managed to send money to his family in Cairo. Then martial law was lifted. That ended the reason for hiding out. If Father returned to Cairo he was not likely to be sent back to jail. But my parents' lives were marked by another personal tragedy during this period. Shortly before September 1945, their second child, Rawia, died from a fever. There had not been enough money for a doctor or for the sugar to sweeten her drinking water, which would nourish her and prevent her dehydration. She was only ten months old. Later my father would recall this incident with sorrow in an interview.

Father returned to his father's home in Cairo and to his wife. For the next few months, until January 1946, he would continue to work with Hassan Izzat. During this period, however, he also renewed contact with Egyptian revolutionaries, notably Hussein Tewfik. Tewfik, who did not belong to the Muslim Brotherhood, had battled English soldiers and had worked against the government while Father was in jail.

Tewfik and a brother announced their intention to assassinate Egyptian Minister Amin Osman, whom they referred to as the "British dog." Osman had said that the relationship between the Egyptian and British governments was "like a Catholic marriage"—impossible to dissolve. Tewfik and his brother evidently thought that the assassination of Osman would help break up that "marriage."

During this period my father joined various parties to explore the possibility of advancing the national political cause. As much as he believed in the liberation of Egypt, my father did not approve of murder as a means of accomplishing this. However, Tewfik and his colleagues proceeded with their plan to kill Osman. The finance minister was entering the headquarters of the Revival League, a political party formed by Osman, when Tewfik shot him.

On the night following the assassination, Father was arrested again at his home. That was January 1946, and it marked the beginning of a thirty-month incarceration. Tewfik and his group alleged that Father had been involved in the planning of the assassination. Eventually, Father would be cleared, after a trial that captured the nation's attention through the mass media.

·

After her mother's estate was settled, my mother inherited some land. She began selling parcels of that land to hire lawyers to defend her husband. Pregnant and expecting her third child in July 1946, Mother continued to visit her husband, who was now being held in Cairo Central Prison. When their child was born, the birth was a cause for limited celebration, since Father was still in prison. The baby was a girl. Mother and Father gave her the name Rawia, after the other Rawia who had died.

During this period Father's friend Hassan Izzat, who had also been implicated in the Osman assassination plot, was being held in Cairo Central Prison. Izzat received visits from his wife and her beautiful cousin Jihan Raouf, who was attracted to Father. In turn he responded to her charm and good looks. Half Egyptian and half British, she was a striking young woman with light skin, glossy hair, and a captivating personality. Jihan's parents apparently were not aware of her budding infatuation for Father. My mother told me that at the time she did not suspect, either, that her husband had become involved in another romance.

•

During the summer of 1948 Father was tried and found innocent of complicity in the Osman assassination plot. He was released. Mother said that Father spent a lot of time at home with her after his release. One night in October 1948 she suspected that she was pregnant again. The next day Mother announced to her mother-in-law, "Count nine months from today. I am going to be having another baby."

Before the end of the year, Mother told me, Father broke the news of his involvement with Jihan. Mother reacted with rage, she said, when Father announced that he wanted to marry Jihan as well as keep her as his wife. Since Muslim men are allowed to have as many as four wives, the proposal was not an unusual one.

"After eight years of my supporting you, you want to do this to me?" Mother said she told Father in shock. "Being your wife is a right I have earned!" Later Mother said she reluctantly conceded that Father could take a second wife if that was necessary to retain her Anwar as her husband. But she and Father separated in December as a result of their arguments over Father's desire to marry Jihan Raouf. Although Mother thought they would be able to work out a solution, Father stayed away from the household during the next four months.

•

Several months later, in March 1949, a man showed up at Mother's home to serve her with divorce papers. The divorce was already final. In Egypt, when a man seeks a divorce, there is no hearing or trial.

During Father's absence Mother had moved to a small apartment with their children. The strain of having to explain or defend her husband's behavior to her in-laws was too great. She had stood by him during the six years of his imprisonment—out of their ten years of marriage—as well as when he was a fugitive hiding from the government. She had tried continuously to ease his suffering. She had sold her property to keep the family going and pay for his legal defense. And now her husband intended to take a new wife. Only years later would Mother talk about how much that divorce hurt her. At the time, though, she buried her grief inside her.

In his book *In Search of Identity*, Father explained that he spent the four months before the divorce became final "taking a cure" at Helwan, a place near Cairo that is known for its medicinal waters. He said he went there to try and cure severe digestive problems that he suffered due to his imprisonment. However, Gail Sheehy's book *Pathfinders*, which included an interview with Father about his psychological preparation for his 1977 peace initiative to Israel, made me recall a pattern in his behavior. When he confronted serious problems, Father tended to withdraw into himself, focusing his psychological powers on the solution. Once he had focused and found a solution, he would move resolutely. I now see that as a lifelong style of coping that he learned as a prisoner in cell 54 of Cairo Central Prison. He often referred to cell 54 as though the time he spent there led to an experience that transformed his life. Father's coping techniques took on an almost Oriental quality of meditation. I think he needed the time at Helwan to focus on a solution to his problem. That seemed to be the case here as well as in other events, including his long-contemplated decision to go on his peace mission to Israel.

So, in May 1949, Father married Jihan Raouf, the daughter of a Cairo bank clerk. She was a nineteen-year-old beauty. Father was thirty. And, at thirty-one, Mother tried to sort out what had happened to her life.

She told me later that she did not really understand why Father divorced her, especially after she put aside her pride and granted her permission for him to take a second wife. "Tell me, why did you do that to me?" she demanded of her former husband. He replied that Jihan's parents would not permit her to wed a man who already had a wife. Later, when I myself had just got married, I felt able to ask his reasons for the divorce. I had heard people speculating about his divorce and remarriage. Some thought he had found a love match. Others saw it as his attempt to become a "modern-looking" politician.

"*Naseeb*." One Arabic word, the equivalent of *destiny*, was the only explanation father would give. The word is used by Muslims to imply that God makes all important decisions, and no human can change what the Creator has decided for him. But it also can signal that this is a matter that the speaker does not wish to discuss.

There was great sympathy for Ekbal, especially since it was her husband who had decided to end the marriage. But Mother did not waste pity on herself. A devout Muslim, she believed that if she was good and patient, her Creator would return her Anwar to her. But although he did not return, she never spoke a word against her former husband and forbade anyone else to do so in her presence. And ever since the divorce my mother kept my father's memory alive in her home, filling the rooms with pictures of him.

In 1972, my mother would finally make her first pilgrimage to Mecca, in Saudi Arabia. When she returned she was elated. The religious experience in itself was uplifting, she explained, but Mother had another reason, which surprised us all. "I am at peace in my heart now," she told us. "I wanted to go to Mecca so that I could tell God that I forgive Anwar and Jihan for what they did to me, and to pray that God also would forgive them." Our great God always urged his creatures to be forgiving and said no human is more noble than one who is known for his forgiveness.

Until that time, Mother had not even spoken to us, her daughters, about how much she had been hurt by Father's decision to divorce her. Afterward, she also told me that on Judgment Day, according to the Muslim prophecy, God will call up all his creatures from the dead. Married couples will be reunited, the husbands with their wives, their first wives. "So," she finished with a radiant smile, "I shall have him for eternity."

Mother was not completely isolated after the divorce. Fortunately, she had family in Cairo—her brother Refaat Madi and his family, her uncle Rashed Mackawi and his family, as well as Sit el-Barein. She also counted on the moral support of other friends, among them the two women who used to travel with her to Maqusah Jail, Lotfa and Rahma Said. Those two became lifelong friends. During this time Mother diverted her thoughts from the divorce by preparing for the birth of her next child in July 1949.

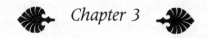

Chapter 3

MY EARLIEST MEMORIES

ON JULY 10, 1949, Mother, whose labor had begun, was attended in her bedroom by her doctor and other women. Her gynecologist, Concetta Damico, was also her friend and landlady. Sit el-Barein held one of Mother's legs and tried to comfort her, and another woman held the other to give my mother something to push against. The labor was long and difficult. Eventually my mother's brother Refaat, witnessing the difficulty, rushed to get his Koran. My mother lifted herself up and he held her around the middle from behind as he recited from that page of the holy book which had fallen open on her lap. When he finished reading, my mother's contractions began to increase in frequency as the child started to fight its way out, and I, Camelia, was born.

Mother recalled that at the sound of my first cry she looked up and saw the horrified faces of those who surrounded her. "Everyone looked so strange," Mother said, "that I wondered whether I had given birth to a little monkey." One of the women reached behind Mother's shoulders and helped to lift her into a sitting position so that she could see the baby. "Then I saw you, my own dark girl," she said.

"Well, someone should cut the cord," Mother reminded Concetta, laughing.

Concetta was visibly upset. "I wanted a boy for you," she explained.

Dr. Damico, Sit el-Barein, and the others had been anxiously praying that my mother would give birth to a son, because according to Islamic law, if a woman who has conceived prior to being divorced by her husband has a male child, the divorce is nullified.

"Well, what are you going to do—put her back into my womb and try for a boy?" Mother chided.

Father came to see his third daughter. He looked at me and then joked, "Why did you carry her for nine months? She looks over-done." In fact, I was the only one of Father's seven children who inherited his dark complexion. "And she looks exactly like me!" he exclaimed happily.

Mother did not hear from her former husband again until January 1950, when he was back in the army—a lapse of about seven months. Although he had given her money when I was born he sent no money during that time for the support of his former wife or their children. In 1951 Mother learned that her husband was in Port Said, Egypt, having a good time. It really seared her soul. A relative who learned that news wrote angrily to Father's captain: "He has made no payment to his first wife and children, though he himself report-edly lives comfortably. Something should be done."

The note evidently produced results. Father came to visit his first family. Mother said he was angry. According to what she has told me my father was angry because he had been under pressure from his superior officer to pay support to my mother for the care of his first family. However, he did pay. And he resumed monthly visits to the family in my mother's home. It was obvious that the cost of support-ing two families in Cairo on a relatively meager income weighed on him. He tried to convince my mother to move and take her children to Mit Abul-Kum. "I would not only continue to support you," Mother said he promised, "but I would also build you a house of your own."

She thought of the future of her children, particularly the educa-tional opportunities they would have in Cairo. My sister Rokaya, ten, attended public school at that time. Rawia, five, was not in school. I was only two years old. My mother valued education, as did her family. A movement had begun in Egypt to promote educa-tion for women. It had been growing since 1919. By 1928 the first group of Egyptian women to go to secondary school earned their degrees. By 1933 the first group of women students to attend the Egyptian university graduated.

Mother recently told me she hoped her daughters would become doctors—one of the few major professions open to women in 1951. She reasoned that our future husbands might leave us, as hers had done. With a profession, we could support ourselves. Mother evi-dently respected medicine as a profession, partly because of her friend Dr. Concetta Damico. Concetta was also such a close friend to my mother that she refused to accept rent during this time, while Mother was having money problems.

In the back of my mother's mind was another concern, she said. Her brothers had already insisted that she should remarry. Living in the village meant that the pressure would be relentless. She simply did not want to remarry. He is trying to punish me, she thought, shaking her head sadly.

Father insisted, "Life in the village is cheaper. If you want to live here in Cairo you cannot live as well." He had a knack of putting things in a way that suggested benefits to the person he was trying to persuade rather than to himself. But Mother stood firm against his persuasive efforts. She would not leave Cairo with her children.

Other things occupied my father's mind in 1951. He began an active role in the Organization of Liberal Officers, sometimes referred to as the Free Officers, in which Gamal Abdel Nasser acted as the "godfather." Nasser and his colleagues were preparing for a revolution.

My father and Nasser had known of each other since 1939, when they both attended a training course for officers. Nasser selected Father for the Free Officer's Organization because of public recognition of his anti-British adventures. At five feet ten, my father was not a small man. Nasser, though, stood about half a head taller. The self-assured and handsome Nasser had a ready movie-star smile. But he also had piercing eyes. Acquaintances recall that they had trouble looking at him face-to-face. His gaze intimidated them. Nasser's body at this time reminded one of an athlete's—broad shoulders and a barrel chest tapering to a narrow waist. Until he became Egypt's president, Nasser usually dressed in a uniform. As president, after 1954 he always wore suits and was always carefully groomed. Nasser never appeared in sporty outfits or shirt sleeves.

Nasser had not been so eager a year earlier for Father to become involved in politics. When, in 1950, news came that Father had been reappointed to the military, Nasser welcomed him back but advised him not to be identified publicly with politics because of his prior political problems. No doubt, Nasser did not want additional problems for his Free Officers' group. My father had not been involved with the Free Officers while he was being held in connection with the Osman assassination.

In 1951 Nasser realized that the Free Officers' Organization needed leadership. He did not hesitate to call upon my father. Anwar el-Sadat was one of seven colleagues asked by Nasser to head the organization. The association brought Father and Nasser closer together. While Father was not overly active in meetings, Nasser increasingly consulted him prior to making important decisions. In turn, Father supported Nasser's initiatives before the group. Nasser had a special appreciation for those whom he could trust. In addition, my father became a key communications link in the organization. He created informational bulletins and arranged distribution so that outlying units of the Organization of Liberal Officers, which was another organization that contributed to the revolution, would be kept current.

The main goal of the organization was to purge Egypt of both its corrupt king and the British occupation that supported and, to a large extent, manipulated him. The target date was November 1955—four years away. Unexpectedly, things took a positive turn. In 1951 the Egyptian government terminated the Anglo-Egyptian Treaty, in effect since 1936. In reality, it had little impact, since the British did not leave. The British were like a self-proclaimed friend who moves into one's household but refuses to leave even when it becomes clear that the welcome has expired.

Public frustration increased following a massive and destructive uprising known as the Cairo fire, which showed there was a sizable opposition to the king. The Free Officers moved up their deadline.

My father focused his persuasive efforts on King Farouk's physician, Yusuf Rashad, who had the king's ear and confidence. Father's object was to attempt to neutralize the king until the revolution could be carried out, but the king was more astute than anyone had guessed. He responded by trying to shore up his support with the military. An attempt was made to inject a key board of military officers with a majority of non-royalist officers, but the king foiled the plan.

In July 1952 the revolution was close at hand. The Free Officers' leaders hoped to use the American government to help keep the

British in check. Besides, the leaders believed the United States supported liberation and social justice. The Free Officers, hoping for U.S. understanding or endorsement, sent a delegation to the U.S. embassy to announce that a revolution was imminent. My father would later write in *In Search of Identity* that the U.S. ambassador was hospitable, even inviting the delegation to dinner. Meanwhile, he said, the British were trying to uncover the names of the principal leaders of the revolution.

On July 23, 1952, the "White Revolution" that would depose King Farouk started. Nasser's colleagues were alerted. Anwar el-Sadat went on Cairo radio to announce the revolution. He also gave the prime minister a set of demands from the Free Officers. The king accepted. Mohammed Naguib, a senior military officer, became the president of Egypt. The next problem concerned King Farouk. Nasser was insistent that the king be deposed and exiled.

Father and President Naguib flew to Alexandria, where Farouk was staying in one of the presidential palaces. They delivered the ultimatum that the king resign and prepare to leave Egypt. King Farouk was hardly a strong political figure, but he refused. His opponents moved their troops and surrounded the palace. Farouk agonized through the night, and the next day, on July 26, 1952, he gave in. He announced that he was surrendering his kingdom but that his baby son would become his royal successor. Farouk began to pack, and a yacht was arranged to carry him into exile.

At 6:00 P.M. that same day the deposed king boarded his yacht. Films of the event showed my father, resplendent in his military uniform, watching the royal yacht slip its moorings. His expression was curiously solemn in view of the victory that had been won with such ease, a victory that would mean a new era for Egypt.

Deposing the king was one thing, but getting rid of the British was another. After the revolution, the new Egyptian government declared that England should remove its military presence from the country immediately. The British began to comply in 1954 but did not complete the evacuation until 1956.

•

For the family, the period 1951–53 represented a status quo. Father continued to visit periodically, and the support payments kept coming. Happily for Mother, the pressure to live in Mit Abul-

Kum lessened. In 1953 Father arranged to have my mother and her brood moved to a larger apartment in Cairo. The building stood a few blocks from our old place as well as from my grandparents' home. I never liked the new apartment. Because the building was located on a main road, I could not play in the street. As a four-year-old, I found that to be very frustrating. Moreover, our old home had been surrounded by a big garden, where I played with a boy cousin.

I thought of my cousin as my brother, because when we were young his mother and my mother breast-fed both of us. Under Islamic law, that fact made us so close that we could never marry each other. My cousin lived in an apartment downstairs in my building. I adored him so much that I tried to act like a boy—even standing up when I used the toilet. Mother would beat me for making a mess.

The new apartment did have one advantage for me. It enabled me to escape the owner of the other place, Dr. Concetta Damico, who used to harass me. Although Concetta delivered me, it was many years before she accepted me. She had seen my mother suffer when my father was in prison and even more when he divorced her. Consequently, she was upset when I was born a girl. She also found my dark skin entirely too much to accept. Concetta would bellow, "You black heathen. Top of a stove! I will kill you if you touch my flowers." Later she came to treat me better and to regard my daughter as her granddaughter.

My first memories of Father are from the period after we moved to the new apartment. Father would visit his brother Talaat, who lived in our area of Kobri el-Kobba, and then stop by our home. He was always dressed in a suit and tie. I remember that one day Father visited our home first, and I pleaded with him to take me with him to see his parents and Uncle Talaat. When he gave in, Mother put me on the dining room table and started changing my clothes. Father waited at the table. As we started to leave I begged him to carry me on his shoulders. With a smile he lifted me to that lofty perch. Then, looking up at me, he said, "How like a little monkey you are." I giggled. Snuggling against him, I sniffed his delicious cologne, which I learned later was called Lavandre Duchesse.

Part of the domestic tranquillity of Sadat's first family might be attributed to the whirlwind of activities in which he took part. In addition to his work with the Free Officers' Organization, he established a newspaper, *Al-Gumhuriah* (*The Republic*) in December 1953. It represented the revolution and was popularly referred to as "the tongue of the revolution." Father became its editor-in-chief. He continued in that post until 1958, in addition to assuming important government duties. His role as the communications specialist of the revolution was expanded. In addition, with his memoirs of his experiences as a political prisoner turned rebel, he showed promise of becoming a prolific author.

As the years passed, he would write eleven book-length manuscripts, the last two of which were to be published posthumously. Among them were *Unknown Pages from the Revolution* (1955), *Secrets of the Egyptian Revolution* (1957), *A Revolt on the Nile* (published in both Arabic and English, 1957), *The Story of the Arabic Unity* (1957), *My Son, This Is Your Uncle Gamal* (1958), *Popularity Base* (1959), *The National Union* (1959), *The Complete Story of the Revolution* (1961), *In Search of Identity* (1978), and *My Will*, published posthumously in 1982. Another manuscript that he had under way at the time of his death, *In Search of Peace*, was being edited for eventual publication.

The first seven books were dedicated to explaining to Egyptians the goals of the revolution, what the new government intended for the people, and the principles of the revolutionary movement. After being ruled, in the main, by others for four hundred years, the citizenry had been conditioned to obey rather than seek involvement in or control of their government. My father's books were designed to awaken their interest in self-government and to motivate participation.

Father's own intellectual inquisitiveness was shaped in part by advice from Aziz al-Masri, the political leader whom members of the liberation movement had failed to help escape by airplane. Father recalled that al-Masri gave him this advice: "Rely upon yourself. Education is important—but not necessarily degrees and certificates. It is important for you to read in every possible field, exploring all directions." My father took that advice seriously throughout his life. I remember that his home always had many books.

He also mastered languages. Father began to learn English as a child when he attended the Coptic school in a village near Mit Abul-Kum and mastered it through further studies at the Royal Military

Academy. During one of his imprisonments a fellow prisoner taught him to read and speak German in about nine months. Years later, Father was proud when Henry Kissinger, then the U.S. secretary of state, allegedly said he pronounced German better than he, Kissinger, did as a native-born German. My father also learned Persian and spoke some French.

After my father became the editor-in-chief of *Al-Gumhuriah*, he paid frequent visits to us in our new apartment. Despite the fact that his office was in downtown Cairo, he would drive fifteen miles each way to be with Rokaya, Rawia, and me. A year later, in 1954, he became the Egyptian minister of state. As a result, all of us, including my mother, moved closer to my father's home.

Those were our glory years. Father seemed to take Rawia and me everywhere. Rokaya did not accompany us because she believed she was "too old" to be tagging along. I particularly remember our weekly trips to Mit Abul-Kum. Father always went on Fridays. The first large check, 400 Egyptian pounds, which he received from *Al-Gumhuriah* for his editorial columns, he donated to the village to build a mosque. He enjoyed praying there with the villagers—a practice he kept up till his last days.

Father attended the prayers, then ate lunch. Afterward he went to El Dawar, the village's principal meetinghouse, to talk with the villagers and hear petitions. Villagers asked him to intercede with the government to put them on the list for financial subsidies that would enable them, as it had others, to travel to Mecca. Often they got the requested aid without knowing that it came from my father's own funds. In his adult life, Father was the most prominent figure in Mit Abul-Kum, and was always welcomed as a son of the village.

Father instructed me in the ways of proper conduct by example, as I saw him interact with the people in the village and with members of my family. He was very traditional. When he met one of his parents he would take a hand and kiss it as a sign of respect before conversation. When he was seated and elders entered, he would rise to honor them. He did not smoke in front of others, or cross his legs, and he did not try to gain advantages over others. That conduct reflects basic Muslim values.

My mother also taught us the same courtesies, since she, too, grew up in a traditional family. I still remember Mother kissing the

hand of her mother-in-law, Sit el-Barein. They both expected traditional, respectful behavior from their children, though they did not
make a point of demanding it. I, too, kissed the hands of my parents
when I met them. As an adult, I never smoked in front of them. My
father expected the traditional expressions of respect from my sisters
and me.

The village truly fascinated me, but my mother did not approve
of my going because she was always concerned about the dust, flies,
and diseases to which I would be exposed. When I returned from
the village she would immediately steer me to the bath. However,
Father generally approved of my contact with the village. On the
way to and from Mit Abul-Kum he talked to me about many things,
including rural life. "You must not be angry with people who behave differently," he instructed me. "These are simple people. Many
of them are your kin." Peasants along the way offered us hospitality
and tea. Father accepted, acknowledging their kindness. My mother
would have grimaced, thinking of the conditions under which the
tea was prepared.

Years after my visits as a child to Mit Abul-Kum with my father, I
got my own car and returned whenever possible to stay at my uncle
Fat-hy's home. I attribute my own love of the village to what my
father taught me about it. Also, even as I write this, I remember life
there before the modernization and electrification. Somehow, the
moon and the stars seemed brighter then, as I peered at the night
sky through glassless, wood-shuttered windows. The glow of electric lighting has diminished that brilliance. Yet the sweet fragrance of
the jasmine blossoms that wafts through the bedroom windows has
never faded.

The family visits continued. Sometimes Father and Jihan visited
my mother's house. At other times we children visited Father and
Jihan and their new daughter, Lobna, at their home. As children
Rokaya, Rawia, and I never quite grasped the significance of Father's
divorce, since it seemed he was always with us. He and my mother
treated each other kindly—more like brother and sister than as a
man and woman who had been married. Father never failed to let
us know that our mother's word was law. "If she breaks your neck
for doing something wrong," he said, "it is my job to get the doctor—not to ask why she did it." Mother similarly imbued us with

respect for our father. "Who are you to question your father?" she would ask angrily when we began to express grievances.

Uncle Esmat, Father's youngest brother, was the only relative from Father's family who visited us regularly. He was always funny and loving. He acted like a second father to me. Our uncle remained close to my mother as well as to us children. When one of us appeared distressed about something, he would say, "Baby, what is wrong?" And if we needed anything he would reach into his pocket, even if it meant giving up his last piaster.

In 1954 Father enrolled Rawia and me in the German school in Cairo. Rawia had been attending an Arabic school. I was five years old at the time and Rawia was eight. For a time we went to school by bus. Sometimes Father sent his own car. Later he arranged a VW "Bug" and a driver to transport us to and from school. Since we had never had a car, this was a tremendous luxury.

During these years, full of energy, I would go down to the street to ride a rented bike with boys from the neighborhood—but only boys. I did not like to be with girls, especially Rawia, who was always sitting with a doll, combing its hair. Playing with boys was more lively. I enjoyed marbles and dancing. Laughing and making noise seemed the natural way to behave.

Mother would swat me and insist, "You are a girl!" But that did not change me. Even my father had trouble reforming me. He caught me riding a bike one day and ordered me to quit playing in the street. I did, then I went to the fourth floor of my building and rang the neighbors' doorbells on every floor all the way down to the basement. It was a wonder that the neighbors put up with me. But I was treated as a favorite.

At school I was good at everything, which was curious because I never did my homework. Hans Anders, my class teacher, said of me when I later visited him in Germany, "Very charming. Bright. First to understand. But never did your homework." Many of these things changed as I grew up. Still, it took me a long time to get over the feeling that I would have preferred to have been born a boy.

•

In addition to his job at *Al-Gumhuriah*, Father became the chairman of the Islamic Conference. He worked a few blocks from our school. Often he picked us up at school, and we visited his office.

The building fascinated me. An old royal palace, it was big and had many fruit trees, including mangoes. It was a treat to visit because members of Father's staff would give us sandwiches, candy, and drinks. Those were good times.

"If you do your tasks and complete your schoolwork," Father would say, "I will send my car and you can be with me at *Al-Gumhuriah*." That was another treat. The newspaper was situated in downtown Cairo. When we did not find something to do in his office, Father would assign an aide to accompany us to window-shop and get sandwiches.

Father's political involvement did not always bring good things. At about this time we discovered that he had assigned bodyguards to accompany and protect us. There had been a crackdown on the Muslim Brotherhood following the revolution. Some of the members of the organization had been executed. The brotherhood had vowed retaliation, including death threats.

That was a miserable time for me, because I valued my freedom. I liked to play in the street, which the bodyguards did not want me to do. I liked to ride a bicycle, and they did not like that either. I would disappear and the bodyguards would call on my mother to locate me and bring me back. I could defy the bodyguards, but not my mother.

·

In 1956 Egypt was attacked by Britain, France, and Israel because their interests were threatened by the nationalization of the Suez Canal. Concerns for our safety led Father to send us to Mit Abul-Kum.

The war arose out of complications related to the Nasser government's plan to build the Aswan High Dam. The government considered the building of the dam necessary to stabilize the supply of water from the Nile River and make possible predictable year-round crop irrigation. Nasser believed that if Egypt could produce enough food, it could offset the problems associated with a surging national birthrate and even provide food to export.

Egypt had counted on U.S. and world banking interests to help finance the Aswan project. However, on July 19, 1956, John Foster Dulles, the U.S. secretary of state under the Eisenhower administration, declared the Egyptian government bankrupt. No financing would be forthcoming for the dam, he said. Nasser's government decided that funding could be obtained through the nationalization of the Suez Canal, then jointly owned by the British and the French. Those two powers gave Nasser an ultimatum. They told him he had twelve hours to reverse his decision or face military action. Nasser refused categorically. The British and French, joined by Israel, which was concerned with access to the canal for transport, attacked Egypt.

The Nasser government asked the U.S. ambassador to seek intervention by the Eisenhower government. On November 5, 1956, Eisenhower insisted on a cease-fire and immediate withdrawal. On December 23 the British and French complied. The Israeli forces did not complete their withdrawal until March 1957.

We spent two months in Mit Abul-Kum with Mother's brothers. The war seemed distant. I soon realized that the village vendors had candy. If you did not have money they accepted barter, such as corn. Mother would not give me money to buy the candy because she feared fly-borne diseases, and the candy was open to flies. Nevertheless, I sneaked out of the household with something I knew I could exchange for the candy. Mother would be enraged and threaten punishment if she found out. But I continued. What she did not know could not hurt me, I reasoned.

If I did face punishment I could count on my paternal grandmother, Sit el-Barein, who had accompanied us to the village. She wore the traditional covering over her hair and a black dress with a long, full skirt. It was big enough for a child to hide under—which is exactly what I did when fleeing from my mother. Grandmother always had a soft spot in her heart for me. Arabs often call cherished ones "my eyes," implying something especially dear. When I was troubled she always noticed. "Grandmother's eyes," she would say lovingly, "what do you want?"

Rawia was also with us in the village. She tended to stay indoors. The opportunities to play with village children did not appeal to her as much as they did to me. After breakfast it was the custom of adult members of the family to sit in the large living room and receive visitors until noon. Rawia would be found sitting there like a little old lady.

Often I would come in from play covered with dirt and mud. I feared Uncle Fat-hy, Mother's younger brother, in whose house we were staying. It was not that I had any real reason to fear him, but he was tall and had sharp eyes. And when I passed by him in my usual grubby state he was usually sitting by the entranceway and would jokingly swat at me with a stick he carried. I can still hear the swoosh of that stick as it cut the air.

I reached the point where to avoid passing Uncle Fat-hy and his stick I would sneak in the back way. I discovered a passage where dry corn was stored horizontally and found that I could scamper over it and get into the house—except the time I fell through the pile, causing me much consternation. Later I would emerge clean from within the house. Uncle Fat-hy would feign puzzlement and ask, "Now how did you get by me?"

Fat-hy's wife, Amina, was a very tall woman. She had a loud voice—I heard it often enough, especially on those days when I managed, in ways known only to children, to get dirty enough to require three baths. Each time, Amina would patiently heat water on the stove, then she would bathe me. She would thump me half-playfully as she washed me, saying, "Must you get so dirty so often?" I thought Amina would have liked to beat me since I was so troublesome, but I knew her to be a kindly woman. Also, I knew that Uncle Fat-hy would never allow me to be mistreated.

•

After two months in Mit Abul-Kum we moved back to Cairo. Several months later, in 1957, it was announced that Rokaya, my oldest sister, who was then sixteen, would be engaged to a doctor who was in the army, Amin Afifi. He was thirty.

Girls were not allowed to go out alone with their suitors. Mother did not like to go out as a chaperone, so Rawia and I often accompanied Rokaya and Amin. What a deal! We got to see movies and were treated to chocolates. I do not know about this idea of marriage, I thought at the time, but if it means movies and chocolates, Rokaya will have it pretty good.

Their engagement lasted for about a year. During that period preparations were made for Rokaya's wedding. A dressmaker was hired, and she came to our home to produce a trousseau for Rokaya. It was exciting to see Rokaya trying on new things.

Finally the wedding day came. The wedding was held in the

Officers' Club. Father, Jihan, and their daughter Lobna attended, along with other family members. Gamal Abdel Nasser, father's close friend and colleague, was also there. Famous singers and belly dancers entertained us.

A few months later, toward the end of 1958, a tragic event occurred: my beloved paternal grandmother, Sit el-Barein, died. The news came while Mother, Rokaya, Amin, Rawia, and I were at a concert listening to a famous singer, Abdel Hallim Hafez. Father's secretary, Fawzi Abdel Hafez, arrived unexpectedly and told Rokaya that Father wanted us to leave the concert and join him. The aide did not explain why we should leave immediately. Finally, the bad news emerged.

Grandmother's death was a tremendous shock, for she was loved dearly by her family. She visited my mother's home, as she did the homes of my father, her daughter, Nafeisa, and her son Esmat. Wherever she stayed, the family wanted her to remain for a long time. If she was at the home of one of her family for ten days, a member of another household would appear to demand that she share a similar visit with them.

Even today I still remember my grandmother's visits, her deep voice and loud laugh, and especially her dawn prayers. She prayed for the general welfare of everyone, but she always included a special prayer: "God, please take care of my Anwar, Ekbal, and his children." I still hear her voice in my mind. My father, my mother, and my grandmother always fasted and prayed five times each day.

My grandmother died of a heart attack in her Cairo home. She had not been strong in her later years, but no one suspected that she was near the end of her life. By chance, my father was with her when she died. They had been talking when Grandmother indicated she wanted to go to the bathroom. It is customary in some households for a younger person to accompany an elderly family member to the bathroom, wait, and then accompany him or her back. My father walked with his mother. "As she came out of the bathroom," my father recalled, "she seemed to sway. Then she began to fall. I caught her and began to take her to her bed. She died in my arms. God was kind to me in causing me to be there with her when it happened."

According to the funeral tradition of our people, the body of the deceased is washed in a purification ritual. A member of the family usually does this. Before her death, Sit el-Barein had asked that only one person wash her, and that was my mother. Mother spent the night at an aunt's house, where my grandmother was laid out.

The funeral was held in Mit Abul-Kum. The family and other mourners gathered at Uncle Fat-hy's house. Father arrived, as did Gamal Abdel Nasser. My mother, who had lost not only a mother-in-law but a friend and a supporter, busied herself with preparations to take care of the family and those who would visit to offer condolences. As a strong Muslim believer, I do not think she cried—at least not in public. Our religion instructs that we should not cry more than one tear or demonstrate grief because more will disturb the spirit of the departed.

At eight years of age I did not know what was going on. I did not understand death. I was just told that I would not see my grandmother again in this life. I began to weep. "Stop your tears!" my mother told me. "She is now in God's hands. She is happy and at peace. Be happy for her."

Although we are not supposed to cry, my father's sister, Nafeisa, also wept. And Esmat wept for his mother. My father became upset at the weeping of his brother Esmat, who was expected to be stronger because he was a man. Father asked a friend to accompany the overwrought Esmat home.

There is always a quick funeral for the deceased. Hospitality is then provided for the mourners who attend the funeral. These practices keep everyone busy, mercifully reducing the psychological stress of death and the funeral. After the funeral my mother remained in Mit Abul-Kum for forty days. It is believed that the spirit of the deceased remains earthbound for that time. Mourners visit the grave and read passages from the Koran. Pastries are baked and given to the poor, according to custom, so that they will pray to God for mercy for the deceased.

•

Early the next year, 1959, my mother was scheduled for surgery. The operation lasted for four hours. Father waited. He arranged first-class accommodations for Mother, even air-conditioning. He visited her often. Father's solicitous behavior toward his former wife generated the rumor that he had remarried her. He could have had more than one wife. Obviously, though, there was no truth in the rumor.

Soon after Mother's operation Rawia and I found our nanny crying and packing our clothing. We learned that we were to be taken to live with Father and Jihan. Though my father's actions obviously disturbed her, Mother said nothing. Legally, father had custody of us, and he now chose to exercise his custody. I think he did it to suppress the rumor and protect his reputation and that of his second family. Throughout his life, my father always acted decisively to protect his public reputation when he believed it under question or attack.

Rawia was thirteen and I was ten when this happened. I began to cry. Rawia cried even more than I did. Fear did not cause our response, it was uncertainty. "Does that mean we cannot see you?" we asked Mother in alarm.

"No," she said. "I will be here." That reassurance helped, but it did not banish our anxiety. Father spoke soothing words, too, but that did not calm us.

Mother insisted on keeping her apartment so that we could visit. Sternly, Father refused. He even insisted that her landlord cancel her lease. "If you return to Mit Abul-Kum," he offered, "I will build you a new home." Mother refused. She was not going to be away from her children. And she was not going to be subjected to pressure from her brothers to remarry. She had decided that long ago.

For the second time, Mother's insistence on remaining in the city, close to her children, caused Father to cancel his support. He knew that she had sold her land and jewelry to care for the family while he was in jail. It was a harsh way to treat her. Despite the pressure, Mother arranged to live temporarily with a cousin until she could find another place. She was always a determined woman.

Finally the car came to pick up Rawia and me. We were about to enter a new phase of our lives in a house that, while it was familiar, did not represent home to us.

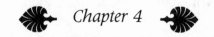 *Chapter 4*

LIVING WITH FATHER

RAWIA AND I were cordially welcomed to my father's home in 1959, both by my father and also by his wife, Jihan. I remember that shortly after our arrival Jihan invited us to her room for a discussion that was designed to establish certain house rules. The main point concerned our older sister, Rokaya, who on various occasions complained to my father that she felt she was being mistreated by Jihan.

"If you have problems with me," Jihan advised us, "then come to me. My husband never hides anything from me. If you go to him to talk about me, I shall surely learn . . ." The implied consequences were left like a sword hanging above our heads. If we crossed our stepmother, we thought, the results would be almost too dreadful to imagine.

Coming out of Jihan's room we looked at each other, talking only with our eyes. This was the first time, I think, that Rawia and I actually sympathized with each other in any situation, for when we were living with my mother it seemed to me that there were always different rules for each of us. I can hear Mother's voice: "Camelia, do not do that. You are still a child. Rawia can do that because she is your older sister." The two of us used to fight a lot because of that difference in treatment. However, Jihan had given us both the same ultimatum. This situation strengthened the sisterly bond between Rawia and myself. Whatever our grievances about Jihan, we could not express them to Father because he would surely tell her. Similarly, if we entrusted Jihan with our complaints about Father, she would certainly tell him. It was better for two sisters to trust each other. And that we did. Countless hours were passed talking behind the closed door of our room.

Yet we were not isolated. We came to know Jihan's sister, Dalia, and her brother-in-law, Mahmoud Abo Wafya. Also, we came to cherish Jihan's father, Safwat Raouf, and his wife, Gladys. Jihan's parents were like a United Nations in human form. The father was of Egyptian and Turkish extraction, the mother was of Egyptian, British, and Turkish lineage. Fortunately for Rawia and myself, all four were warm and affectionate—and they lived nearby, just off the garden of my father's house. A visit meant a quick trip across the garden and through an opening in the boundary fence.

Jihan's father was concerned for us. One day when we were getting ready to go to school, he addressed his daughter in our presence about her responsibilities. "What is it, Daddy?" Jihan asked when he broached the topic. (Being partly British, Jihan spoke the word *Daddy* in English quite naturally.) "These two are like little orphans since they are separated from their mother," he said. "Remember that you must take care of them now."

I remember Safwat Raouf as an open, friendly person who was always cheerful. My father's car and chauffeur took him to his workplace, where he was a clerk in a real-estate bank. In turn, he was a self-appointed shepherd for the youngsters in the family, who were also transported to and from school in the same car.

Dalia and Mahmoud, Jihan's sister and brother-in-law, opened their homes and hearts to us. Somehow I knew that if I stayed around in the kitchen to pick at food that was being prepared I could count on an invitation to share whatever the family had to offer at mealtime. So luckily Rawia and I found other havens of comfort.

As weeks turned into months, my father seemed to be living under some strain. It was not because things were going badly for him politically, however, for he had become the speaker of the Egyptian parliament. A heart attack that my father suffered on May 15, 1960, at age forty-two, after we went to live with him and Jihan, seemed to rob him of his confidence in his ability to provide for his family. At that time he had only the house that he and Jihan lived in and his monthly salary. He had taken out a loan to finance the house. He earned about 150 Egyptian pounds (about $600 then). His income supported a house of six children. He gave no support payments to my mother after he took Rawia and me. She said he gave her 500 Egyptian pounds (about $2,000) when he had taken Rawia and I to live with him and explained, "That is to compensate you for what you spent on me while I was imprisoned." In the mid-1960s he would resume payments to my mother and continue them until he died.

While we were living with him my father once said that if anything happened to him his pension would be sufficient to keep Jihan and her children in the house and support them. That plan did not include Rawia and me. Father was worried about the welfare of the children of his first marriage. He wanted us to have reasonable security and the chance for an education.

I think his concern for Rawia and me grew out of his personal experiences. During the period when he opposed the British and after his commission in the military was withdrawn, he lived a harsh, impoverished life, one that had little of the compensating warmth and fascination he had found during the early years of his life in Mit Abul-Kum. Moreover, he had always placed a high premium on education, largely because of his own hunger for knowledge and the difficulties he had in getting a formal education as a youth after his family's move to Cairo.

The father who had laughed and joked before he took us to live with his new wife had became solemn, stern and more than a little short-tempered. He often struck out at almost anyone, including Jihan, for what seemed to be silly reasons. "Jihan, why were you at Dalia's?" he would demand irritably. "Camelia, go change that dress," he would order. "Hassan, is this iced tea? Get me hot tea," he would bark at his personal servant. Poor Hassan. He was responsible for Father's clothes, food, and his room. Hassan was so upset that he brought a small stove and put it next to Father's room so that when he asked for hot tea, it could be served boiling, as Father liked it.

Father also experienced pressure from malicious individuals who circulated rumors that he had remarried my mother, Ekbal. After separating from my mother, Father had kept two houses for his two families. He never thought of having the two families live under the same roof as some traditional Egyptian men might. It was when the rumors started that he decided to close the second house and take Rawia and me to live with him.

When my father's behavior began to change I worried that I might be to blame. Father usually laughed often and was warm and sweet. Now I found he did not kiss me as often and rarely took me out with him. He even stopped calling me by the nickname Camm-ool (little Camelia) that he and my mother used. Not knowing what had changed Father, I began to feel that this was his way of punishing me for something I had done wrong. I did not ask Father both because I lacked courage and because of the tradition that in households where the parents live together children go to the mother for advice. Mother was not there, and I did not feel I could turn to Jihan again, because she usually dimissed my protestations with the comment, "That is his nature." Also, I was afraid she might tell my father and he in turn might believe I was criticizing him.

Father did not talk much to Jihan either. However, what went on behind the closed doors of their rooms we did not know. In an Egyptian household such things are private, even from the other members of the family. My father also went out alone a lot. That was not unusual for Egyptian men since they tend to leave their wives and children at home except when attending movies, family events, and celebrations. However, it marked another change in my father's behavior. He lived a rather insular life at this time, apparently fighting his personal devils.

During this frustrating period the only times I saw the father I used to know was when he slept or read in the garden. Once, early in the morning, I passed his room en route to ask Jihan for my daily pocket money for school. Father never closed his bedroom door. I looked in and saw him sleeping. He lay on his side, with both hands tucked under his pillow, one knee drawn up to his chest. His usually stern face was clear and serene, like a child's. I stood at the doorway looking at him for as long as I dared, treasuring this rare glimpse of him. After that I frequently tiptoed past his room early in the morning, trying to catch a glimpse of him before he awoke. At other times I found him reading in the garden, one of his favorite places to relax. He loved being in the open. Even when the temperature soared to 110 degrees Fahrenheit he would be there. He did not like being cooped up. And he did not like refrigerated air. Later, for example, unless he had visitors with him, Father almost never used the air-conditioning in his car.

Rawia and I were not completely separated from our mother during this period. We were allowed to visit with her every other weekend for two hours. As for Father's relationship with my mother, the truth, as I know it, is that Mohammed Anwar el-Sadat loved Jihan completely, but he also held some reserve of affection, mixed with respect, for my mother, Ekbal. They had been through much together during the emotionally turbulent years of his early military career and imprisonment. The psychological bonds between husbands and wives that are forged in fires of adversity are not weak, and they are not easily broken. Yet his love for Jihan made her in many ways the real day-to-day ruler of his household. For example, Jihan would not have my mother, the first wife, enter her home. To the end of his life, it was that way. My mother, on the other hand, welcomed Jihan in her own home on occasional, brief visits and when she attended my sister Rokaya's engagement and wedding ceremonies.

In many ways my father was a traditional Egyptian man. He allowed my mother to be the day-to-day disciplinarian of their children. He would always withdraw from family disputes but at the same time made it clear that he supported my mother completely. If life was tranquil he would be tender and loving. Often when he came home he would inquire, worrying, "Did you have dinner yet?" Many nights he would slip quietly into the children's rooms to pull up or tuck in our bed covers. When we children sneaked into his room in his absence to watch TV and unintentionally fell asleep, he would wake us gently, saying, "Do you want to go to bed now?" No reprimands were forthcoming. My father predictably deferred to the women of the household in certain spheres of decision making. Above all, he had a deeply rooted sense of obligation to his families.

•

In 1961 Rawia was fifteen years old and I was twelve. We had been living with my father and Jihan and their children for two years. Rawia and I were still dumpling-like little girls. Though younger, I stood about an inch taller than Rawia. Physically, we had passed over the line that divided girls from women. Mentally, Rawia acted her age. But I still had a child's attitudes and energy. In the household we were both treated more like adults than children. We helped care for our younger half sisters and half brother. The household refrigerator had a lock, but Jihan entrusted Rawia with the key and she in turn helped feed the younger children. I washed the youngsters and also told them bedtime stories. By this time my father and Jihan had four children of their own—Lobna, nine, Noha, seven, Gamal, the only boy, six, and Jihan, also known as Nana, one. My other sister, Rokaya, then twenty, lived with her husband.

·

Early in the summer of 1961, in July, a major in the army who was then thirty-two years old had asked my father for Rawia's hand in marriage. She was then fifteen. Her suitor, Galal Gomaa, was seventeen years her senior. In Egypt it is not uncommon for a girl to be married early, depending upon the custom of her family. In rural Egypt, where Father was raised, parents marry off young daughters to lighten their own household expenses and ensure the future of their daughters. Egyptian law requires the sheikh who performs the ceremonies to make sure the bride is sixteen years old, but the practice is sometimes circumvented. All of us were happy that Rawia would be beginning a new stage of her life and become mistress of her own household.

At that time we left Cairo to stay at Father's beach house. The heat and dryness of Cairo made escape to the beach house a welcome prospect, and we stayed there until the end of August.

In September someone knocked at the door of Father's house in Cairo. I opened the door impatiently, for Father and I were supposed to go to a movie—something I had been anticipating as only a twelve-year-old can. Standing in the doorway were two men. "We would like to speak to Mr. Sadat," the older one said. "Please give him this card."

I turned and headed toward my father's bedroom. If they had only come five minutes—just five minutes—later, I thought petulantly, they would not have found us. We would have been on our way to the movie. Now we would surely miss the film. I was unhappy. Not only would I not be able to munch on pumpkin seeds—the Egyptian moviegoers' equivalent to popcorn—I would be denied a family outing. Being out with Father, Jihan, and the other children in the family gave me great joy. Even now as an adult living far from my relatives I am miserable at the thought that I cannot take part in family gatherings.

As I approached my father's room I glanced at the visiting card. It belonged to my grandfather and bore his handwriting: "Carrying this is General Gamil Attia Abdelbary. I worked with him in the Sudan. He is a good friend, and his son is a fine young man."

I entered my father's room and gave him the card. "How long will these people be here?" I asked, growing more restless as I thought about our outing to the movie. My father gave me a look, a mixture of puzzlement and exasperation. "Open up the big room to receive the two guests," he said and I did as he instructed.

A few days later, I was sitting in my room when Rawia entered. She looked unusually serious, almost angry. "Father asked me to tell you that you are going to get engaged to the man that came to visit last week," she announced flatly, and it was now clear that she was angry, she was upset that she would be sharing her moment of glory, her engagement, with her younger sister. Rawia had been unhappy away from Mother and had welcomed me as her confidante and ally, but our new friendship ended abruptly that day. Rawia would not answer any of the questions that rushed to my head and soon left me dazed but a little excited. This was a new adventure for a twelve-year-old.

The arrangements were to be changed with what now seems to be amazing rapidity. My father's first plan was that both Rawia and I would have a two-year engagement. By then Rawia would be seventeen and I would be fourteen. But Rawia's fiancé objected. He did not want to wait two years. Next it was proposed that Rawia be married in October and that my engagement be announced at the wedding. Finally, my fiancé, Ezz Abdelbary, suggested that Rawia and I be married on the same night.

My father did not object. He responded with a Muslim saying that is something like, "The good is that which God chooses." If there were no impediments, then, it was taken that God had smiled upon the planned marriage and that it was the beneficial thing to do.

The main obstruction to getting married in Egypt is usually lack of housing for the new couple. Recently, the problem has become even more serious in urban areas like Cairo, resulting in longer and longer engagements. However, in our case it was not a real obstacle to a quick marriage.

Everyone seemed happy—that is, everyone except my mother, who did not even know that Ezz Abdelbary had asked for me in marriage. Years later my mother told me how upset she had been when she learned about the plans for my sister and me to be married at such early ages. "When your father took you away from me," she said, "it was as though he took away my power. He could take you without my consent since he had legal custody. And because he had custody, he could plan your lives without consulting me. I felt defeated." When Mother finally learned about the wedding plans, Father did not even choose to talk to her directly.

In my father's household everyone was elated about the pending marriages. "You are going to have your own husband and your own house," a servant said happily. Egyptians tend to get wrapped up emotionally in the lives of others—sharing in festive occasions, making joyful trilling noises at weddings, and sharing in the grief at funerals—and it is always from the heart.

I did not really know what marriage meant other than the simplistic perspective of a twelve-year-old. I had a dawning awareness that it meant that some things I liked, I could do. Perhaps I could avoid things I did not like. "Will I have to get up early?" I asked. Not necessarily, came the reply. That was good. Early rising was not something I liked. "Will I be able to go to school?" I asked. Yes, came the reply. That was good, too.

I toyed with thoughts about what a married woman should do. My main thoughts were about being able to wear high heels, going to the hairdresser, and, most important, wearing makeup. I began to ask Rawia how to apply eye makeup. She sneered, saying, "Do not be presumptuous! Your husband might never allow you to use cosmetics. Anyhow, you are only going to get engaged. Stop dreaming!"

One night I was dancing around in the privacy of my room, singing to myself and practically flying. My mind was running through the benefits I would have as a married woman. Not the least of them was the liberty to do what I wanted. I was more than a bit headstrong when my autonomy was involved. For example, while I was living with my mother I desperately wanted a bicycle. I used to rent one by the day from a neighborhood entrepreneur for a modest charge. My mother was angry. Riding a bicycle was not an activity suitable for a young girl from a traditional Egyptian household. Mother was concerned with what is appropriate conduct. I did not see why it was all right for boys to ride bikes yet not for girls to do the same. However, my mother's voice rings with the conviction of firsthand experience with the holy Koran. Despite her expressed will, I wheedled until a friend rented a bicycle. In exchange for some "trade," I would get the use of the bike, putting miles on it in hours. The deception in the rental was necessary, since not even the man who rented the bicycles would risk my mother's wrath once he learned that she had forbidden me to rent a bike from him. I must admit that while I respected and revered my parents, I was in some respects a willful child who put a high value on personal autonomy. Because marriage promised to release me from the close scrutiny of my elders, I equated it with personal independence and thus welcomed my impending liberation.

My father later summoned me to discuss my engagement. It was the first time we had spoken together about it. When I entered his room, he was talking on the phone, and I stood with my head down, looking at my feet, as though counting my toes repeatedly. While waiting I glanced about. I used to see my father's room mainly at night when I sneaked in to watch the only TV set in the house. His was the northern room, and in summer it had the best breeze during the long, hot Cairo nights. The room was big yet simply furnished. The bed, which was quite big, was to the right, and to the left was a closet. The TV was across from the door in a corner where two comfortable chairs and a small table were located. It was the biggest of the four bedrooms in Father's house. As I finished scanning the room my father looked at me. He was smiling. If there had been any doubt in my mind about the marriage, which, theoretically, I had every right to refuse, it was banished by the obvious pleasure I saw in my father's face. I would have done anything for one of his smiles and if getting married made him happy, I would do that. Then he spoke to me. "Now you must behave as an adult," he said, suddenly serious. "You are an adult. You are not a child anymore." Then he began to discuss buying a wedding ring for me. I felt a surge of excitement. "You can pick out the ring you like," he said. "I will pay for it. It can be whatever you want." His face softened. Out of the corner of my eye I noticed the change in his countenance. I beamed. The luxury of having a ring appealed to me. And perhaps more important was the fact that my father seemed to be trying to please me, taking my preferences into account.

In Egyptian families it is not unusual for the father to buy his daughter's wedding ring. Ostensibly it comes "from the husband," but sometimes it is bought as a token of love from the father or as a way of maintaining family status when the fiancé or his family cannot afford a more elegant purchase. In this case, I believed it was a sign that my father, who had been emotionally distant since I entered his new household, really had not withdrawn his love from me. At the moment I felt he would give me anything I wanted. As I looked at his calm face I thought I had rediscovered my sweet, loving father again and I was happy.

"You may go to your room now," my father said. The smile was fading from my memory. I was being dismissed, but the glow of the moment carried over. Back in my room I relived that moment with not a small degree of rapture. I considered running back to his room to hug and kiss him because of the happiness I felt. I did not, though, because I knew I would be told that women should not act that way. Trapped between childhood and a premature introduction into adulthood, I did not know how to vent my feelings.

The news of my impending marriage irritated Rawia, who had basked in the attention that followed the news of her own engagement. For a time after Father's news about me she reacted with pique because she thought that, intentionally or unintentionally, I was stealing attention that rightfully belonged to her. She huffed, "Children are going to marry?" (She meant me.) "Unbelievable." She tried to boss me around, threatening, "If you do not do what I say I will tell my father and you will not get engaged." Somehow, Rawia could not even accept the idea of my engagement until the jeweler showed up with a collection of rings for me to inspect.

The engagement party followed the next week. It was a small affair and did not last for more than a couple of hours. My fiancé came with his family this time—his parents, three sisters, and four brothers. From my side, other than Father, there were only my sisters, Rawia and Rokaya, and Rokaya's husband. I could not resist teasing Rawia, "Did you see my ring?" Rawia just looked at me with an unbelieving stare.

Yet Rawia and I got past all of that when we went with Jihan to the dressmaker's to design our wedding gowns. The two gowns were of the same design, as though Rawia and I were twins, and we loved them. Jihan was happy. She began preparing drapes for my apartment and crocheting things to put on tables and chairs. She took Rawia and me shopping for furniture.

My father seemed happier now that his second and third daughters were engaged. He smiled more and talked in a different way—like someone who had shed a great weight from his shoulders. He invited Rawia and me to share lunches and dinners in his room. Father had never done that before.

During this period I did not hear from my mother at all. She knew only that before the summer vacation Rawia had become engaged. Because of Jihan's feelings toward her, Mother was not invited to the house to share in the planning of the weddings. Perhaps because my father did not care to confront his strong-willed former wife, he did not even choose to communicate with her directly. To Rokaya, the eldest daughter, who had been married for four years and had her own home, he said, "You tell your mother that Rawia and Camelia are to be married. Tell her that she can see the children at your home after the contract is signed." This was done two or three days before the wedding.

I did not know anything about sex in marriage. In Muslim households mothers were supposed to explain their daughters' transition to womanhood. But Jihan said nothing about that aspect of marriage, and I did not know enough to ask.

The little information I gained about sexuality came from an elderly servant named Hana, the wife of our gardener. It almost scared me out of my wits. I remember the look in Hana's eyes, which seemed to say, "Well, child, that is the way things are." Hana and I had drifted into a conversation about my impending marriage when we got into a matter-of-fact discussion of the wedding night. "The bride is taken into a room, away from the other guests," she told me. "There, female members from both families place the bride on a bed and hold her legs. The husband wraps one finger with a white cloth, then inserts it into 'that place.' If it comes out stained with her blood, it is known she is still a girl. The father of the bride and the other males wait outside. The father stands at the door. If the cloth shows blood, the husband passes it to the father, who takes it on a stick and walks around for all of the family and guests to see. It is a sign of honor for the bride's parents."

The ritual she described was evidently ages old. For the bridegroom and his family it obviously gave proof that the bride was not tainted merchandise. For the parents of the bride, it was proof that they had raised a virtuous daughter. In matters of lineage and property, under the eyes of religion it was evidence that any children issuing from the marriage would, indeed, be those of the husband.

However, for me it was a horrifying prospect. My traditional upbringing had, in a large degree, isolated me from the realities of sexuality. Even the movies were careful not to unveil the mysteries. Egyptian society tends to shelter young girls, prolonging their innocence. Also, the separation of young boys and girls has been a given in Muslim society. Therefore the notion that anyone would see and exploit my body was unthinkable to me. Also, as I have said, I valued control over my own life. The tradition that Hana described to me demanded the ultimate surrender—giving up personal control of my own body.

The impending signing of the marital contract brought the dreaded wedding night closer. The fact that my prospective husband did not have our apartment ready—it lacked furniture, drapes, and household necessities—was something of a blessing. My mind did not dwell constantly upon the vision of the virginity-certification ceremony, but it was never far from my consciousness, especially when I became aware that my wedding day was at hand.

·

The day of the marriage arrived, October 10, 1961. It was an unusually solemn occasion—especially in contrast to the usual Egyptian wedding, which is festive and even boisterous after the wedding contract has been signed. Guests drink sugary non-alcoholic beverages, eat, talk, watch dancers, and make sport of the bride and bridegroom. They also make loud trilling noises with their tongues as a salute to the newlyweds. But not in the case of Rawia and myself. Father was a political figure, and even our wedding became intertwined with what he viewed as a tragic political event that took place at the same time.

In 1958 Syria and Egypt had joined to form the United Arab

Republic. It was a sign of strength and unity in the wake of years of colonial rule in the Middle East. For various reasons the pact that united the two countries broke up a few days before the wedding. Clearly, my father viewed this as a national tragedy. "There will be no music, no party, no celebration," he vowed. Not even for his daughters would he make a concession. "No one can be happy in view of what has happened between Egypt and Syria," he said morosely. But the wedding, itself, would go ahead.

At the wedding, except for Jihan, her sister Dalia, Rawia, Rokaya, and myself, all of the other participants in the ceremony were men. That few women attended was in keeping with my father's idea of solemnity in the face of Egypt's political crisis. Among the men were brothers of my mother, Salem and Mohammed, who was now *omda* of Mit Abul-Kum. At least there was a symbolic attempt to represent her side of the family at the wedding. Jihan's father and brother-in-law were also in attendance.

As is the custom with many Muslim weddings in Egypt, Rawia and I did not acually attend the main part of the ceremony, when the wedding contracts were signed. Often the bride asks her father, another family member, or someone she wishes to honor to represent her in the contractual part of the ceremony. In this case my father honored his father by asking him, Mohammed el-Sadat, to represent both Rawia and me.

In the ceremony, if both the man and the woman are present, the sheikh instructs the bride and bridegroom to join hands and covers their hands with a white handkerchief. He then invokes the blessings of Allah, then reads the first sura, or verse, of the Koran. Next, he asks the bride if she will take the bridegroom as her husband. If the reply is affirmative, the bridegroom is asked if he will accept the bride as his wife. After the bridegroom accepts the handkerchief is removed and the parties move to the signing of the wedding contract.

During the ceremonies Rawia and I waited with other women in a room upstairs while our grandfather gave the appropriate responses. Before writing the marriage contract the sheikh is required by Egyptian law to demand proof that a bride is at least sixteen years of age. In Rawia's case it was a pro forma matter because she was so close to being sixteen. In my case, the law provides that if no birth certificate is available two persons of unquestionable repute may examine the bride, then certify that she is of marriageable age.

The two persons in this case were my father's longtime colleague and friend President Gamal Abdel Nasser and Marshal Abdel Hakim Amer, the military commander in chief in the Nasser government. As required, they certified to the sheikh that I was "of age." Since a girl under twenty-one years of age cannot sign a legal contract for herself, our grandfather signed for Rawia and me. The wedding contracts were then concluded.

At that point, had things gone according to normal form, a servant who had been at the signing of the contract would have gone into the hall to make a loud trilling noise, which would have been the announcement to all who waited that the wedding had been concluded. However, because of my father's insistence on a solemn event, this was omitted. At age twelve, then, I became a married woman with a husband who was seventeen years my senior. Rawia was also married. She was nearly sixteen, and her husband was also seventeen years her senior. Although Rawia was the older, with high-heeled shoes our heights were about the same. We were an attractive pair of brides.

The wedding party seemed more like a funeral party since few, if any, women attend Muslim funerals. Also, the participants were standing around stiffly, as though their bodies had been starched. The presence of Gamal Abdel Nasser contributed to the dour atmosphere. Nasser was a person of stern visage. If he did not smile, no one around him dared to do so. To me, though, President Nasser was a dear uncle with humor and considerable patience. When I was younger I would jump with pleasure when Father said we were going to visit him. A visit always meant fun for me. The presidential home had a big garden with two mulberry trees. The guards would caution me, but I would shout back, "Don't worry. I am used to climbing trees from when I go to our village." Mother was not so charitable. She would punish me if she caught me climbing trees, so I did not mention it to her. Nasser's wife, Tahia, would leave me playing in the garden and only call me in for food.

Nasser came over to congratulate me on the wedding, and as he smiled broadly, another scene flashed into my mind. When I was six my father and I were having lunch with Nasser, his wife, and his daughter Hoda. I was sitting on the table and Nasser nodded to my father, indicating that it was okay. Across from me was a caricature of the president emphasizing the prominence of his nose. I began to sing, "Uncle Gamal has a beak! Uncle Gamal has a beak!" My father, shocked, cried, "How dare you say that? Get down off the table immediately." But Nasser seemed amused. "Come on, Anwar. She is just a child," he said. Then he turned to me and asked, "Now tell me, who taught you this song?" "No one," I replied. "It is my song." He then asked, pointing to his nose, "Then how do you know this is a beak?" "Mother told me," I replied. "When I asked her why it was so big she told me, 'It is not a nose. It is a beak.' " Nasser was laughing, but my father's face had a tortured look. That was the last time he ever took me to President Nasser's home. Even my mother punished me for my childish behavior.

As Nasser looked smilingly into my eyes on my wedding day I wondered whether his smile reflected his happiness or the memory of that incident at his dinner table. At the wedding party he politely partook of the sweetened beverage that is traditionally served at Egyptian weddings and the candy-coated almonds. Photos were taken. Then he said his good-byes and vanished into the night.

After President Nasser left, the wedding party loosened up a bit—but not much. It did not seem festive at all—certainly not as a marriage should be. Rawia's husband, Galal, looked distinguished in a dark suit and tie. Ezz was dressed in his army uniform and wore a cap perched casually on his head. Perspiration stains were beginning to show under his arms. Perhaps he was as nervous as I was.

Ezz does not look beautiful, I thought, but he is nicer-looking than Galal and does look handsome in his uniform. Ezz was about five feet eleven inches tall, but he looked shorter because he walked with a stoop and tended to bury his head between his shoulders. He looked at the floor and tended not to look people directly in the face, so I could not catch his eye. At the time army officers were considered good catches. Their earnings were two to three times that of college graduates, I was told. Also, in the war movies I had been watching, the lucky girl always married the dashing army officer. There was great passion. But, unfortunately, the dashing young officer usually got killed at the end of the movie. I hope we have better luck, I reflected.

At the end of the ceremony, I remember, people were smiling ridiculously. Now I realize they were trying to express their solidarity with a somewhat confused twelve-year-old girl. But at the time I remember thinking, They are making fun of me. Why are they making fun of me? We will be going out soon, I said to myself. Then I started remembering movie scenes again. I will put my hand on his arm and he will escort me out, I thought. In Cairo, when couples walk on the street you can always tell the sweethearts from the married couples. Sweethearts hold hands. A wife puts one hand on the husband's arm. I looked at Rawia, who refused to look at me. She was still upset with me for sharing her show.

Soon we were heading down the steps of my father's house to a waiting car. I hurried as fast as I could, for I was going to see my mother, whom I had not seen for months. Rawia, with tears streaming down her cheeks, was still saying her good-byes to Father and Jihan. She was kissing Jihan. My two stepsisters, Lobna and Noha, cried out, "When are you coming back, Rawia? We want to come with you." Rawia paused to hold their hands and calm them with promises that she would soon return to visit them. "Come on, Rawia," I called impatiently. "We are going to be late. Mother is waiting!"

Soon Rawia and I and our husbands were swept away by car to Rokaya's house. There our mother awaited her two newly married daughters following the joint wedding ceremonies from which she had, in effect, been banned.

As the luxurious auto rolled to a stately stop in front of Rokaya's high-rise apartment building, a welcoming party greeted us at the curb. Among them was my mother, statuesque and dignified in her long evening dress, Rokaya, neighbors, and even the doorman. As Rawia and I maneuvered our way from the auto, taking care with our billowing dresses and veils, I saw that my mother was crying. Everyone pressed in around, us, offering words of enthusiastic congratulations.

We were buoyed along, Rawia and I, to the central elevator, which had glass on all four sides. At each level, until we reached the fourth, where Rokaya's apartment was, neighbors appeared at the landings to greet and cheer us. Finally we were secure in Rokaya's apartment with our beloved mother. It was a happy reunion.

Soon Galal, Rawia's new husband, began teasing Mother, asking, "Do you have your bag packed to go to Alexandria?" In Egypt it is customary for the mother to accompany the new bride and bridegroom home when they will be living far away. She helps prepare meals and in general eases the transition for her daughter. Also, the daughter knows that she has a member of her family to turn to for counsel and comfort during the first hours of being in her new household. Since he came from a village near Mit Abul-Kum, Galal was fully prepared to follow through with the tradition.

"No, no," exclaimed my mother. But Galal persisted. Then Mother's face brightened into a smile. Anyone who admits respect for the old ways has taken several steps toward making an alliance with my mother. "Well, I do have some things with me," she confessed almost shyly.

Everyone enjoyed sitting around the dinner table. The table was filled with delicacies that my mother had prepared. Ezz did not speak much, except when, with a mouthful of food, he thanked Mother for giving him an extra serving of this dish or that.

"When you move to your house, Camelia, I will teach you how to cook," my mother said. That was when I realized that for my husband food was more important than socializing. It would later become one of the really important things in his life.

As the evening drew to a close Rawia prepared to depart for Alexandria with Galal and my mother. At that moment the numbing day of activities and the strange new sensations caught up with me and I felt alone and afraid. Rawia, whom I had teased and bedeviled mercilessly when we were younger, had become my friend and closest confidante as well as a cherished sister. The two years in my father's house had bonded us in a way that neither time nor distance could undo. When she went out the door, though, I felt, that the separation was one of the great tragedies of my young life.

My own husband, Ezz Abdelbary, had not yet completed the arrangements for our apartment and I was to return and live in my father's house for another three weeks. Although that would provide me with some degree of comfort, it was a time of increasing trepidation about my new role as wife.

•

When Ezz and I moved into our own home in 1961, there was a small party to celebrate. That evening would be our actual wedding night. I tried to be composed and charming, as was my duty. But I could not help noticing Ezz's relatives and thinking about what Hana, the servant, had said. It seemed to me that something was sure to happen soon. Apprehension lurked beneath my calm exterior. Finally one of Ezz's brothers came toward me. Although it is obvious to me now that he intended to touch me and greet me as his new sister-in-law, what I saw was the first step in the dreaded ordeal. He was going to grab me and pull me into the bedroom, where the others would perform the ritual. As he reached out I went flying into a nearby room, slamming the door and locking it behind me. "Camelia? . . . Camelia?" he yelled through the door. "What is wrong? Camelia . . . ?" There was confusion and frustration in his voice.

"Go away!" I yelled back. My heart pounded wildly. "I know what you want to do to me!"

Only then did I learn that Ezz and his family did not hold with the old ritual that Hana had described to me. I got my nerves under control eventually. Then Ezz and I were finally alone. I had passed one ordeal and had to confront yet another. I did not know what to expect, but it had been impressed upon me that I had a duty to perform. The Muslim view is that the woman exists to satisfy the needs of her man, to give him children, and to serve him.

If I knew virtually nothing about sex, I suspect that Ezz knew little more. Whether or not he had been with a woman before his marriage, I do not know. There was nothing like touching or affection in our coming together—not even kissing. I was terrified. Moreover, I thought what was happening to me was dirty. I felt forced to submit, though, because my elders had continually stressed the virtue of obedience. It is believed that if you are not obedient God will not accept you as a good person. The obligation of obedience more or less enslaved me to my new husband, who was almost two decades older than I.

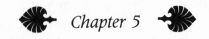

Chapter 5

A TWELVE–YEAR–OLD
GROWN–UP WOMAN

THE DAY AFTER MY WEDDING NIGHT, my father came to visit, to show his affection and help my marriage get off to a good start. In Egypt the father's visit is also customary for another reason. If, in the absence of a virginity-certification ritual like the one Hana described, the new husband finds on his wedding night that his bride is not a virgin, he has the right to order her father to take her home the next day. My father had nothing to fear on that count.

He came to bring wedding gifts of cash for me. "Here is something from me," he said. "And here are gifts from your Uncle Gamal" (Gamal Abdel Nasser) "and from Uncle Hakim" (Abdel Hakim Amer, father's friend and Nasser's military commander in chief). I received three presents of about 100 Egyptian pounds each. It was more money than I had ever seen. My father seemed satisfied that he was giving his daughter such a good send-off. The gifts overwhelmed me. Although I did not fully understand the magnitude of the money, I felt deeply that my father cared for me and wanted nothing but good for me.

My father kept smiling as I looked at him and I wondered why. Was he laughing about what Ezz and I had done the night before? Was he covering his shyness about asking me? I could not help wondering what my father and mother did on their wedding night. Did he do to my mother what Ezz had done to me? Did what Hana described happen to my mother? I still found it difficult to accept what I had experienced in the marital bed. Considering the way I had been raised, I thought it was naughty—and painful.

•

I began planning my role as Mrs. Abdelbary, the manager of Ezz's household. This might have been a pretentious way of looking at it considering that we had only one servant, a country woman who dressed in a galabia and wore a veil outside of the household. She washed, cleaned, shopped, and cooked. She knew what to do and consulted me only when she needed my approval.

Our apartment was in Mansheit el-Bakry, a suburb of Cairo, about ten miles from the center of town and seven miles from the airport. Mother and her brother Refaat lived three blocks away. Father had a home about twenty-five miles away on Pyramids Avenue in an area that was residential but now has many nightclubs. Our apartment was part of a new construction area. The planners had experimented with a contemporary, high-density complex of apartment buildings that required fewer maintenance workers than did older Cairo buildings. Our building had six floors with four apartments each; we lived on the second floor. Our place had a formal living room, a family room, one bedroom, a dining room, and a kitchen. There were balconies on two sides, one that looked out on the front of another apartment building and another facing the backs of other buildings. The uniform, uninspired environment seemed sterile to me.

I remembered that Ezz would have a birthday in about a week, so I used my bride's gift to arrange a large party for him. As days blurred into weeks I continued to operate the household with the gift money my father had given me. Soon the funds were almost gone. I went to confer with my mother.

"You used all of your wedding gift to operate the house?" she asked incredulously. "You silly girl! You should tell your husband to give you money to buy food and other things that you need. You are his wife."

I returned home and asked Ezz as my mother had instructed. "You are just a child," he replied. "How can I trust you with money?"

I was a child, and often I acted like one. I used to wait behind the entrance door to our apartment and spring out to surprise him when he arrived home. He did not react, so I gave that up. At other times, when we were walking and I saw children playing soccer in the streets I asked him to wait so that I could watch the game until it ended. Usually he did not want to wait. But the few times he did indulge me by stopping, I yelled encouragement and advice to the players. Before my marriage I had played soccer and liked swimming. My swimming was restricted when I moved into my father's home. He did not want me to go swimming at the beach. "You should not put your body on display for all to see," he said. He meant that I could not wear a bathing suit in public, and I could not even swim in a galabia. It was only after the Officers' Club began to allow women to swim on Wednesdays, when no men were allowed in the pool area, that I was able to resume my swimming.

There were times when having a child's lack of control was particularly distressing. When there was no food in the house I waited for Ezz to come home, pangs of hunger radiating from my stomach. When he arrived I often found that he had stopped to have a meal at his mother's home. Only after my father visited did our house have a supply of food. He came at least once a month when he went to see President Nasser, who lived across the street.

If I grew insistent about money Ezz would give me a piaster to buy something like bread and cheese. But at times he also tried to avoid giving me anything at all. He insisted that I would only waste money and that, anyhow, he was impoverished, living on a military man's pay. I recall that he earned about thirty-eight Egyptian pounds, and I remembered what I had been told about military officers in Egypt being well paid.

As I continued to press my case for an allowance to manage the household, things got worse. First Ezz discharged the servant, contending that we could not afford help. Second he began to beat me. It reached the point where any kind of dispute, such as matters of food or selecting a program on TV, might result in Ezz punching me in the face. If I was not convinced of what he said he would hit me. If I argued back he hit me.

I could cope with the menial labor of running the house without a maid, although in the homes of my mother and father a child of my age would never do such heavy work. A typical home in Egypt requires constant cleaning. At certain times of the year, dust is thick in Cairo. There are no wall-to-wall carpets everywhere to catch and hide dust and dirt until one has time to vacuum. Floors have to be swept and then washed on hands and knees daily. The clothes and bed linen must be washed by hand, wrung out by hand, and then hung out to dry. Frozen and canned foods are far from the norm. Shopping and food preparation must be done daily.

Domestic life with Ezz soon revealed the problems of marriage between a child and an adult. On too many topics Ezz had one perspective and I another. For example, I loved watching TV. In 1960 Egyptian TV had started showing American shows and I loved them, particularly *Bonanza*. It was the first time I realized that real families lived in America as well as whooping Red Indians. "Oh, come on!" Ezz would say. "You are just a child. You do not understand." He did not understand my point of view and did not want to comprehend. He simply rebuffed my comments.

My traditional upbringing helped condition me to accept Ezz's domination. In addition to the general tenets of Egyptian society, I received instruction from my mother, who had herself been raised within a traditional value structure. From the age of eight I was taught how to pray and fast, and how to behave. Moreover, I learned that women existed to serve men and that younger people were to be both respectful and obedient to their parents and other adults. Even today I rise automatically from wherever I am seated when an older person enters a room.

I continued to try to get Ezz to give me money, especially for food. "I am hungry," I said one night.

"Well," he replied, "it is late—too late for a child to be wandering around the markets." He acted as though that closed the matter. But I did not give up.

"We could send the doorman to get some things," I suggested.

"He is gone," Ezz replied. I knew it was a lie because I could hear someone in the doorman's apartment, evidently watching TV. I called the doorman.

"Give him money," I told Ezz when the doorman appeared. Rather than suffer the embarrassment of a domestic quarrel in front of the doorman, he dug grudgingly into his pockets for money and handed it over. I, too, had learned to be devious. It was necessary in order to survive. However, it was not without penalty, because Ezz often vented his frustration by battering me.

I did not conceive that I might protest to others, even to my family, about the abuse I suffered silently for the first two years of my marriage. Like many abused wives throughout the world, I just took the mistreatment. Rarely did I muster enough nerve to strike back when he hit me. My plight more or less escaped my family's attention until my father's younger brother Esmat asked me one day in 1963 about my marriage. That opened the way for me to voice my problems.

I was frank. I told him about being left without money, about having used up my own money, and about being beaten. My uncle was furious. He confronted Ezz. "You are dirt," he said, waving a finger at Ezz. "I would not lower myself to deal with you. You see those children?" he asked, pointing to some of his own small off-spring. "*They* are the ones who will take care of you if I hear more of this from Camelia. They will administer your punishment." It was bad enough to be threatened, but for an adult to be told that he would be put in his place by children is a harsh insult in a society like Egypt.

Word of my uncle's confrontation with Ezz finally reached my father. He called me to talk to him. "Ezz Abdelbary is your hus-band," he said. "You do not carry tales of your troubles with him to others—and especially not to your uncle." He was expressing the basic rule of traditional society. The husband owns the wife, and the wife is not to bring disgrace to her master, no matter what she suffers.

"But he leaves me hungry," I protested. Surely my father would be moved. He could not let his daughter go hungry, I thought.

"Here is some money," Father said. "Take it." Then he cautioned me, "But do not go to your uncle again—or even to your mother."

I could imagine my father's thought: How could I have such a willful daughter? If he had thought about it he might have realized that he sired more than one strong-willed daughter. My sister Rokaya is like dynamite with a short fuse. Rawia, who was shy and retiring as a child, has increasingly stood up for what she believes to be right or necessary. Father had taught us to be independent, and we were exactly that.

Despite my father's refusal to do anything about Ezz's behavior, I would sometimes go to his house to complain to him about Ezz's treatment. I did not achieve any change in my father's attitude dur-ing these visits. But I got pleasure out of seeing my stepmother and her children. Jihan and I shared jokes, and she gave me lovely things. Often she opened her clothes closet and we went through her garments. "What do you like?" Jihan would ask. She would then produce projects for us to do together. She was great at sewing and spent time showing me how to improve my sewing skills, and gave me the materials I needed.

At this time my father was away in Yemen. Having overthrown King Farouk, Nasser's government enthusiastically supported a pan-Arab movement that sought to depose royal monarchies and replace them with republican governments. Yemen, located south of Saudi Arabia, was in 1962 a kingdom ruled by Imam Ahmed. A republican revolutionary movement sought to overthrow his government. Egypt intervened in support of the revolutionary movement during a civil war in Yemen (the Yemeni Civil War). Egyptian troops were sent to aid the revolutionary forces. My father went to Yemen as a political consultant, sharing the organizational and political experience of the Egyptian revolution. He traveled between Egypt and Yemen and in this way preceded Henry Kissinger as a "shuttle diplomat" in the Middle East.

The Egyptian intervention in Yemen was drawn out. It was to last from 1962 to 1967, when Egypt became involved in the Six-Day War. The Yemen intervention did little to improve Egypt's status in the Middle East, for Saudi Arabia, which also has a royalist government, became furious with the Nasser regime. Although Saudi Arabia did not enter the warfare, the United States, as an ally of Saudi Arabia, reduced its foreign aid to Egypt in retaliation.

In July of 1965 I was feeling nauseated and went to my doctor. He told me I was pregnant. I had already had two miscarriages, probably due to the heavy housework I had done after the maid was fired. This time I was determined to keep my baby and lived in daily horror that I would forget my medication or somehow lose it.

Ezz had little enthusiasm for my pregnancy. He did not especially try to belittle my experience, but like a typical Egyptian male he viewed the pregnancy as one of many to come—and therefore no reason for excitement. I have been fascinated by the degree to which prospective parents in other countries become involved in changes in the wife's body, the first movement of the child in the womb, and the kicking of the unborn child. To Egyptian men a pregnancy is as unworthy of discussion as going to the bathroom after a meal.

My father said, "Fine! Finally you are pregnant." What he meant, I think, was that Rawia, who married at the same time I did, already had two sons, Mohammed and Sameh. Rokaya, who had married earlier, had also borne two sons, Mohammed Anwar and Ashraf.

My impending motherhood elated my mother. I am her "baby," so she constantly concerned herself with my well-being. She shared my suffering and my hopes, offering rivers of advice. "Do not clean," she said. "Do not bend over—it might hurt the baby," she advised. "Try and sleep on your back, with your legs elevated," she urged.

Ezz and I continued to fight over money. To keep me quiet, Father gave me money from time to time. Yet Ezz was determined not to give me any more of his money than was necessary. He kept pleading poverty. I think he learned his attitudes toward money from his parents. His mother and father kept money separately and his mother, in particular, was very tight in spending "her" money on anything.

One day I made an eye-opening discovery about Ezz and both his dishonesty with me and his self-proclaimed poverty. He had a box that he kept under lock, claiming that it contained only documents that were important to him. One day for some reason he left the house without locking the box. He certainly must have been distracted, because he had always locked it and hidden the key. Curious, I opened the box and peered inside. There were books inside. I took out the top one and opened it. Each page was folded to form a pocket, and each pocket contained money. Ezz had a secret cache.

I closed the book with the handmade money pockets and returned it to the box. Then I locked the box and put the key away. When Ezz returned home I did not tell him what I knew. I just told him that I had found his box unlocked and that since a hired person was coming to clean, I had locked it and put the key away. His box was safe.

"You did well," he said. But the look on his face suggested his worry that I knew what the box held.

I could not talk to anyone about Ezz's money box. I believed that if I said anything to him he would beat me. I was afraid of him. And a Muslim wife must not embarrass her husband; no one would want to hear me or believe me. Ezz forgot to lock his money box on other occasions, especially when a driver and car were waiting for him, and I got into the habit of locking it for him.

Some things improve with age, but our marriage, like a wine from poor grapes, definitely did not. The strife over money continued. Ezz, infuriated with my insistence, continued to beat me. I felt caught in a labyrinth. Like a rat in an experiment I could run to and fro. Every once in a while I accidentally hit the lever that dispensed a reward—but not often. One thing was certain: there was no easy way out. I wondered sometimes whether and at what point the rat comes to resign itself and accept the labyrinth.

My escape took the form of burying myself in TV romances and films. One day I decided, I am going to love this man, and we're going to have a happy life like they do in the films.

Ezz came home to a surprise. "Kiss me," I urged him. We embraced, and our lips touched—just as they do in the romances. However, in a moment I felt that something was wrong. Our lips were still touching when I opened my eyes. I found myself looking into Ezz's wide-open eyes. He had never closed them. Have you any idea what a strange sensation it is, during a romantic moment, to find you are looking into your lover's eyes at a distance of less than an inch? If fish were to kiss it would be a lot like that. So much for romance.

·

I had been married to Ezz for five years now, and he still did not give me a household allowance or money to pay for my food. We skirmished from day to day over the few piasters it took to feed me. Ezz continued to decry what he saw as my untrustworthiness with money. Once I unintentionally played into his hands. "I knocked over her purse one day," he said to my mother. "What do you think I found? The purse was stuffed with candy." He tried to make it sound like a customary event. Considering the trouble I had getting my hands on even a piaster, it was really quite rare for me to have candy.

One day my mother finally became incensed enough to use her own persuasion on Ezz. Until now Father's warning not to tell Mother about my problems had inhibited me from talking with her. Increasingly, however, I spoke my mind. Mother, who vividly remembered the feelings of powerlessness she experienced when Father took Rawia and me from her household, now seemed to be on my side. "I am your parent, just as your father is your parent," she told me. "I am going to take care of this matter with Ezz." My husband was up against a formidable opponent the next time they met.

"You really should give Camelia a budget to take care of herself and run the house," Mother began.

"She is just a child," he said.

"Well," countered my mother, artfully appealing to Ezz's ego, "she is growing up, and you, as an adult, have to help train her to accept her responsibilities." Ezz, at thirty-four, could not argue with that unless he wanted to admit that *he* was not a responsible adult.

Mother moved into position for the kill. "Let us suppose you give her a weekly allowance. I will help her plan a budget for the week—how much to spend for fruit, how much for meat, how much for bread, how much for soap. . . . Then I will go with her to shop to make sure that she spends your money wisely. Also, you must realize that costs are not always the same. They keep going up. So from time to time you will have to add to Camelia's budget."

With someone so earnest and determined as my mother, Ezz could not say no without suggesting that he did not trust my mother either. It was the triumph of a stronger will over a weaker one.

My doctor ordered me to bed, saying he would prescribe treatment to ensure a successful pregnancy. Thinking about my impending motherhood calmed me, and I was especially thrilled when I felt the baby move inside me. I decided I would try for peace with Ezz. I would begin by convincing him not to beat me again. Then I would do whatever he asked of me. It was worth it, I thought, for the sake of the baby. Ezz agreed when I talked to him, but the truce did not last long. I forgot my pledge to obey, and Ezz got mad when I refused to visit his mother.

Ezz's father, General Gamil Attia Abdelbary, was a kind and interesting person, but my mother-in-law, Hamida, was really a trial. Being with her was like being ground down with sandpaper. She did not like me at all. My color was reason enough for her to attack me. "You black barbarian," she would snarl, "I am going to find a worthy wife for my wonderful son!"

Her husband frequently kept to himself, staying behind the closed door of his room. When he heard his wife abusing me, he came out on the attack. "She is the daughter of your master," he reprimanded his wife. General Abdelbary regarded Father as an important man in the government.

"Are you taking the side of that black monkey against me?" Hamida fired back. Sometimes in such an argument my father-in-law reached down, took off a slipper, and hurled it at his wife's head. I had been brought up to respect my parents and I treated Ezz's parents accordingly. I would never talk back to my elders.

My father-in-law would nod at Ezz and say to me loudly, "Leave that [meaning Ezz] to his mother." Then he would address Ezz directly, "You're getting to be like your mother—sitting in the kitchen and gossiping." Then he would lead me off to a quiet place, where he told stories, often recounting his heroics in the Egyptian army in the Sudan.

Ezz's mother had insults enough to last all day. Also, like Ezz, she was a penny pincher. My mother-in-law and her husband were both financially well-to-do, but they maintained separate incomes. He would pay for certain things while others were her responsibility. She was never eager to spend her money. She was also savage. One day while I was visiting her she beat a little girl who worked for her. When the girl screamed and pleaded to go home, Hamida told her that if she did not obey, she would be burned before she was sent back.

It was Hamida herself who told me proudly one day how she once burned a cat that had taken a piece of chicken she had cooked. She waited until the cat finished eating the chicken, then caught it by the neck, dunked it in the gasoline tank, and touched a flame to the wet animal. The flaming cat zoomed out of the house. Hamida's father saw the blazing animal and called for someone to catch it before it reached the fields and set them afire. Afterward Hamida confessed to her father that she set the cat afire as a punishment for stealing the food. I vowed that day that I would never be alone with my mother-in-law.

When I refused to visit his mother, Ezz ordered me out of the house. My mother lived a few blocks away with my uncle. That was the first time I thought of going to her instead of to my father.

My mother, too, believed she should not interfere in husband-wife matters. She calmed me down, but then said, "Camelia, it is very late now. You have to go back to your husband. If your father hears that you have left your husband he will get upset." Mother led me back home that night without saying anything to my husband other than, "Ezz, here is your wife. She is safe." She left without even entering my house.

The time for my baby's birth came. It was March 12, 1966. Ezz and I had been married since 1961. All the events leading up to the time of the delivery were a blur in my mind. As the anesthetic wore off I awoke to Dr. Maher Mahran's voice. "Why are you crying, my daughter? We did not do anything to you!"

Dr. Mahran had done a marvelous thing for me. He had delivered my baby safely. God had heard my prayers for a girl. Both Rokaya and Rawia were in England when I had my baby. Rokaya had gone to live in London with her husband, who had received a scholarship to work on his Ph.D. During her stay she had a miscarriage, and Rawia went to London to help take care of her.

"Ekbal, of course!" That's what I replied to my mother when she asked what I wanted to name my daughter. When my sister Rokaya had her first son she named him after my father, Mohammed Anwar, and I decided I would honor my mother by naming the first granddaughter for her. My mother was thrilled, but she was worried that the name might offend my father.

"I do not care!" I exclaimed. "You are my mother. He is my father, but if this embarrasses him that is his problem."

In fact, Father came that evening. He had just returned to Egypt from the United States. The Yemen intervention had affected Egypt-U.S. relations adversely. "In foreign relations we were now at a point of direct confrontation with the United States," Father was to write in *In Search of Identity*, "and, as Nasser always went to extremes in conducting a dispute, he pushed this one right to the point of no return, relying as he did on Soviet support." Yet the U.S. government invited my father, as speaker of the National Assembly, to visit the States. He was received cordially. He was even invited to the United States Congress. Father saw all of this as a U.S. effort to explore the possibility of a rapprochement.

When Father arrived and learned that he had his first granddaughter, he asked the baby's name. I answered, "Ekbal."

"You named her after your mother," he said, pleased. "Great!

This is very good, Camelia," he continued. "Your mother must be very happy."

In all honesty I had not considered naming my child for anyone other than my mother or whether anyone's sensitivities might be touched. But I unintentionally offended Jihan. Jihan neither called me nor came to see the baby at the hospital. When she finally saw my daughter she said, "You must have had a lot of pressure to name her after your mother. . . ." I realized there was no way that she would accept that it was my own idea.

I was to think of this many years later when my stepsister Noha had her second child, a girl. While visiting her in the hospital I asked what Noha planned to name her new baby. Noha's husband, Hassan, said, "She was named Jihan. Shortly after the doctor presented Noha with her daughter Jihan held the baby in her hands and said, 'You are Jihan! Oh! My little Jihan.' " Jihan was flattered to have a child named after her. She had young cousins who were named after her. Also, her last child, my youngest stepsister, was named Jihan. I did not realize how important this was to her when I had my own child. But even if I had, I do not think it would have changed my decision. My mother stayed with me at my home for two weeks to instruct me and help with the baby.

•

Later in 1966 Father called me and my sisters Rokaya and Rawia to his home. This was after Rokaya and Rawia had returned from London, where Rokaya's husband, Amin Afifi, had been studying in a graduate program since 1963. Father announced that he wanted to tell us his decision about the division of his property in the event he should die.

"I paid for Rokaya's marriage and bought her a home," Father said. "I think I have also done well by you, Rawia and Camelia. I arranged for your security by helping with your marriages, and I also got furniture for you." Then he continued, "Jihan and her children also need their security. I propose that the city house will be hers. My village house and its land (about fifteen acres) will go to Gamal. It will be open to all of my daughters."

The whole issue meant very little to me at the time. I suspect that no teenager spends time anticipating her father's death.

My baby daughter occupied my days and gave me great pleasure.

Having Lulee—my daughter's nickname means "pearl," and that is what I usually call her—changed me almost overnight. My mother benefited because I used to argue with her, especially when she tried to advise me about anything. I was at peace with myself. I even found myself going to Mother and asking her to forgive me for the pain I had caused her over the years, promising to try never to make her unhappy. Until then, I had never really understood how much she had suffered, what a strong woman she was, and how her family had become her life. "I shall never remarry," she said. "I have to keep my family together." But I have always believed the real reason my mother did not remarry was that she loved my father so much that she never wanted another husband after him. She was the type of woman who existed for only one man.

My thoughts also made me aware of the beauties of the mother-daughter bond. I recalled the nights I had slept with my mother. I would press up against her in the bed, putting one leg over the notch formed by her waist. It probably woke her up a million times during my childhood. I thought about how much pain my mother had probably endured in giving birth to me—though, knowing her, I'm sure she never cried out, because that would have cost her her dignity. I began to see how she had stood up under the weight of her problems as woman, wife, and mother. And I wondered whether I would ever be able to match my mother's success.

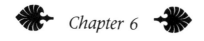 *Chapter 6*

CONFLICTS WITH FATHER

DURING the latter part of the 1960s the Egyptian government was caught up in a series of critical political events that would occupy much of my father's time.

Nasser's government had moved Egypt into the center of Middle Eastern politics when it nationalized the Suez Canal, then maneuvered the United States into forcing France, Great Britain, and Israel into pulling back after their military retaliation. A number of other Arab nations regarded Egypt with increased admiration for having stood up to major world powers. Building upon this, Nasser worked to develop a pan-Arab movement, which would be recognized as the United Arab Republic. Egypt signed a pact with Syria in the late 1950s, but that agreement collapsed after two years. The Nasser government also supported efforts to rid the Arab nations of royalist governments, a policy that led to the Yemeni Civil War, which lasted from 1962 to 1967. It soured Egypt's relations with the royalist government of Saudi Arabia and also led other Arab governments to regard Egypt cautiously lest it intervene in their political problems as well.

In 1966 Israel and Egypt moved toward a confrontation. Israel launched a raid on Jordan. In 1967 Nasser, then the head of the pan-Arab movement, requested the withdrawal of the U.N. Emergency Force, which had been stationed on the Egyptian side of the Sinai Peninsula since the 1956 war over the Suez Canal. He also insisted that the UNEF troops be withdrawn from parts of Sinai, including Sharm al-Sheikh, at the head of the Gulf of Aqaba. Israel regarded Nasser's moves as the prelude to an attack and cause for war.

The Nasser government was, indeed, preparing Egyptians for war. Government-influenced media editorialized that Egypt was the most powerful Arab state and that it possessed missiles that could reach the heart of Israel in minutes. Patriotic songs urged war. Tele-

vision increased the number of war movies. In all the public activities, though, no one discussed the fact that a substantial part of
Egypt's army was still tied up in Yemen and that intervention there
had drained Egypt's economic resources. In addition, there was a
struggle going on between Field Marshal Hakim Amer, the army
commander in chief, and Ali Sabri, the prime minister, that would
result in Sabri's political isolation.

The withdrawal of the U.N. Emergency Force caused Israel to
deal Egypt a preemptive strike by attacking and destroying the
Egyptian air force on June 5, 1967. They then seized the Golan
Heights from Syria, the Sinai Peninsula from Egypt, and occupied
Jordan's West Bank, with a view to taking over Jerusalem. This
became known as the Six-Day War. An estimated ten thousand
combatants were killed in those six days. The Egyptian military was
devastated. Nasser felt that in view of the magnitude of the defeat he
should resign as head of Egypt's government. But his resignation
was rejected. Major demonstrations showed him he still had considerable support. As speaker of the National Assembly my father
called that government body into an emergency meeting. With tears
filling his eyes, Father said before the National Assembly that the
Egyptian people were united in their need for Nasser's leadership.
This was typical of Father's loyalty to Nasser, who had appointed
him speaker of the National Assembly, then asked him to step aside
in favor of another Free Officers' member. Father did, and when
Nasser requested that he take the lesser post of deputy speaker, my
father accepted. "I did not really care about Nasser's change of
heart," Father would write much later in *In Search of Identity*. "I
never sought power or a position."

This was a time of great trial for all Egyptians. Their government
in its military defeat had lost its supporters in the Arab bloc. And it
got no sympathy from the major Western powers. However, the
U.S.S.R. eagerly came to Egypt's aid, seeing the country as a Middle
Eastern foothold.

As a central member of Nasser's government, Father had enough
problems to keep him going day and night, so we did not see or hear
from him during these days. What we knew of him came mainly
from reports in the media. Even if Father had contacted us, we

would not have learned much. Father simply did not like to talk politics at home—at least, not with members of his first family.

•

On the second day after Israel began its war with Egypt, my mother came by taxi to my apartment and told me, "You must pack quickly. We must leave and go to Rokaya's house." Mother said Rawia and her children would join us there. "Whatever happens, we will all be together," she reasoned.

When we were united, Rokaya, Rawia, and I all worried because our husbands were all army officers. No one wanted to voice the question that burdened our minds. Would we ever see them alive again? Our mother had always seemed fearless, but in this crisis I learned that there was one thing that did scare her: She did not so much fear for herself as for her family's safety.

A blackout that night transformed the usually bright and bustling Cairo into a dark sanctuary for the alarmed masses. Mother recited again and again from the holy Koran. The sound of her voice comforted us as we three sisters sat silently, out of respect. Suddenly an inexplicable outburst of noise filled the house. Almost at the same time, a toilet began flushing repeatedly without being touched, and Rokaya's maid, who had dozed off, began to snore loudly. We daughters could not hold back our laughter. The absurdity of the noises broke our tension. Mother, though, completed her recitation of a verse from the Koran. Then, unexpectedly, she began to shout. After she regained her composure I asked, "What is it that bothers you so much?"

"During the Second World War we used to get blackouts like these," Mother recalled. "At those times I was always frightened by the sound of the airplanes, never knowing what would happen to us."

In the oppressively hot days that followed, life in Cairo and most of Egypt changed dramatically. People seemed in a daze. Everyone moved as though carrying the burden of a hundred pounds of invisible chains. People worried that relatives, loved ones, or friends might have been killed or injured. There was no information about death tolls. Television programmers eliminated all entertainment shows. Virtually the only news about the war came from international broadcasts. Moreover, Cairo became even more jammed with people as the government declared three cities near the Suez Canal part of the military front and began the evacuation of civilians.

There was no way to block out the war. Evacuees were knocking on the doors of Cairo residences, asking shelter for themselves and their families. And anguished cries from different quarters of residential areas pierced the days and nights as Egyptian families learned that their menfolk would never again return home.

Leaders of some other Arab nations initiated a program of aid to Egypt after the brief war, and the Soviets promised to resupply our military. The Egyptian government closed the Suez Canal to international traffic. The sudden defeat by the Israelis caused a generalized psychological depression in Egypt that generated soul-searching questions among many citizens. Why had Egypt intervened in Yemen? If our military strength had not been split between Egypt and Yemen at the time of the Six-Day War, would our defense have been adequate? Should Egypt have been drawn into a conflict between Jordan and Israel? There were no easy answers.

•

Several months later, after calm had returned to Cairo, the electric company turned off the power in our apartment. That night, in February 1968, Ezz and I argued by candlelight. "Did you pay the bill?" he demanded. Since the birth of Lulee, Ezz had grudgingly given me a small household allowance—as requested by my mother. He still had a miser's reluctance to part with his money. He was sure I had forgotten to pay the electric bill or that I had misspent the meager funds he had given me.

"Yes," I replied. "I am sure I paid the bill." In my mind I was certain. But being right hardly mattered when the lights had been turned off. Candlelight outlined the hard features of Ezz's angry face and cast shadows on the walls of the darkened room. "Take your daughter and leave," he ordered. It was hard to tell why he was so furious. It was midnight. What was I to do? I was nineteen, with a two-year-old daughter. I had no money. Even if I had had money there was little hope of hiring a taxi at that time of night. What would I do?

"I do not care," Ezz shot back when I told him I had no money. "Just get the hell out of here."

I went to a neighbor's home. I was ashamed to tell the truth, so I told her that the military had sent a car and driver to pick up Ezz—which was something that happened occasionally—and that I did not want to be alone in our apartment with Lulee. The neighbor graciously took us in.

The next morning I borrowed money from the neighbor and took Lulee to my sister Rokaya's home. Angry at Ezz, I unloaded my problems on Rokaya. I talked about the verbal abuse, the beatings, the hungry nights, the fights over money. It all came pouring out of me. For the first time, at age nineteen, I thought of divorce. It was 1968, and I had been married for seven years. I am not going to suffer anymore on account of that crazy man, I said to myself.

The way Ezz treated me enraged my older sister. She called Father. We then went to his home, and Rokaya presented my case to him. I mentioned that I was thinking of a divorce. Father decided to call Ezz to talk to him.

I was sitting with Jihan, while Ezz talked privately with my father. My husband was his usual sneaky self in putting his case before my father. Father returned to accuse me with Ezz's words. "Your husband says that you go out without permission," he repeated. In Egyptian society a wife did not go out to shop or visit without first getting her husband's permission. Failing to observe that rule could result in a divorce. "Ezz says someone is playing around with your mind." Clearly, Ezz was suggesting that I might have a boyfriend on the side. If Father had really believed that I was fooling around with a man other than my husband he would not have just shouted at me—he would have killed me, so strong was his sense of religion and honor. By this time Ezz had entered the room. He presented the image of a quiet, reasonable, and long-suffering man caught up in the actions of an irresponsible young wife. "I want my wife. I want my daughter," he said. "I was jealous." As though that explained everything.

Now it was my father's turn to take up the attack against me. "So you want a divorce?" he bellowed. His face was dark with anger, his eyes like lasers. "You leave your daughter here, then," he screamed. "You leave the house. You never come back." Father was as dramatic as an actor in expressing his indignation. His voice rang with conviction.

Jihan left the room after my father told her not to interfere. My mind was reeling. Father's attack had cowed me. Then Father asked Rokaya for some money, which he evidently intended to give to Ezz to placate him. Father rarely carried money and continuously asked for loans, particularly for gifts in unforeseen situations.

Rokaya's temper flared again. "This man beats Camelia and you want to give him money?" she snapped. "No matter how long or what it takes," she told my father loudly, "I am going to show you what a snake he is." Father did not react. When he took a position on family matters he did not usually retreat.

Rokaya was determined that I should not return to live with Ezz and face further mistreatment. "That man is going to the Second Army in a month," she said. Ezz had in fact been called up for extended service with the Second Army as part of an Egyptian preparedness campaign against Israel in the continuing tension after the 1967 war. "Camelia should go now with Lulee to live with my mother," Rokaya continued. "Then everybody will know who is lying and who is telling the truth. Anything she does will be in clear view of the family."

My father looked thoughtful. I suspect he was mulling over the implications of having two divorced daughters on his hands at the same time. Rawia had been divorced in 1966, two years earlier, and Father was paying support to her even though she lived with my mother. If I were to be divorced it would mean paying support to me, too.

My mind was seething with resentment against Ezz. I am going to make him pay for what he did to me I told myself. No more kissing, no more touching, no more sex. Despite all of the fights we had had over the years I had found Ezz engaging and often charming in a helpless sort of way. When he returned home from work I had continued to greet him with hugs and kisses. No more, I said to myself. For the first time I was so angry that I felt I might eagerly batter him physically, as he had done to me—especially for that ugly lie suggesting that I had a boyfriend. But angry as I was, I think Rokaya was even angrier. I think she would have liked to kill Ezz that night.

"She is not going back to that apartment with *him*," Rokaya said, in pointed reference to Ezz. "There is going to be a separation *now*," she insisted.

Father maintained his stern attitude. "You agree?" he asked me rather harshly. I nodded.

"Okay," he said with a final air.

While the argument raged, I struggled with my emotions. My heart was beating rapidly. Run, Camelia, my emotions said. Leave your ugly husband and your father who does not want you. Leave the whole family and run. The insults are too much. You cannot win. I was feeling helpless. The voice of Rokaya shouting at Ezz and arguing with Father resounded in my head like a storm. My emotional tension got much worse after Jihan left the room, for I knew that she could be counted on to defend me.

Rokaya's voice drew me out of my thoughts. "I am going to take care of this situation," she promised. "Just leave it to me. I know you do not really want a divorce. You are just angry because of what happened to you. I know you love your daughter and your husband."

On the way out I thanked Rokaya for trying to understand my situation. "Are you crazy? You are making too much of this," she said. "You are like my daughter. Do you know, Camelia, that my mother got sick after she gave birth to you and was not able to feed or take care of you? I was doing all that. You are not only my sister, you are my first child. I used to feed you, change your diapers, and sing to you. Don't worry. Just leave it to me."

For that moment, at least, I felt secure. I felt that I had someone close to take care of me—someone who had great feeling for me.

Rokaya had her way. I moved into my mother's house, joining her and Rawia.

My mother was no more sympathetic than my father when I tried to talk about my problems. She was not aware that Ezz had been abusing me and also swearing against her in an obscene way. "Are you stupid—or crazy?" she demanded. "Who would take you in if you left him, crazy child?" She pinned me with an intense stare. "Your husband is trustworthy, and he is a wise man."

At first I had a hard time accepting her position, then I began to see a picture of Ezz in my mind—the image he conveyed to my mother. He appeared thoughtful and meek. He rarely lifted his eyes to look directly into the eyes of another. He had recently graduated from Cairo University with a degree in philosophy—and since most military men terminated their schooling with a martial education and never went to college he was an exception in the Egyptian army.

After I moved into my mother's home my anger against my father grew into a tremendous storm. "He is not my father anymore," I muttered aloud. I was determined not to have anything to do with him.

I was so centered on my own problems that I did not recognize that my father was under great pressure resulting from the political furor precipitated by the Israelis' capture and occupation of Egyptian land in the 1967 war. Although we did not know it at the time, Father traveled all over Egypt to meet with leaders of the Arab Socialist Union, the only political party during that period, attempting to explain why Egypt had become involved in the Yemen war. He evidently made trips to every regional government unit in Egypt to meet with party members and shore up support for the Nasser government.

We usually learned about Father's travels from the media. At other times we learned about his political trips only when he returned—and then he shared no details. For example, one day in 1968 Rawia and I visited his home. Father was not there. We were with Jihan and the children when the street in front of the house became filled with cars. Father entered, walking briskly. He had just returned from a secret state visit to the U.S.S.R., where he had attempted to get armaments to resupply the losses sustained by the Egyptian army in the 1967 war. He had brought presents for us. But we were told, "You cannot talk about this with anyone."

Despite the end of the war Egypt and Israel were not at peace. From 1968 until 1970 Israel waged what was called the War of Attrition against Egypt. There were sapper attacks on Egyptian territory. There were air raids. I remember that one attack hit a civilian factory at Abo-Zaabal, in the south of Egypt. Another one damaged a primary school in Bahr, a village east of Cairo, killing a number of schoolchildren. Every day Cairo Radio announced that Israel had attacked again. Egyptians were frustrated because the army seemed powerless to stop the attacks. Our government engaged in counterattacks on Israeli territory, but if they were supposed to discourage the Israelis from further attacks on Egypt, they were not successful.

Meanwhile, other things that had enriched our lives disappeared. Until the 1967 war Cairo had three TV channels. Two carried Egyptian movies and music. The third offered news broadcasts in English and French as well as American television series and movies with Arabic subtitles. I recall that we watched *Voyage to the Bottom of the Sea, The Nat King Cole Show*, and *Bonanza* regularly. *The Invisible Man*, because of its novelty, was extremely popular. After the war, though, the government shut down the third channel, pleading economic problems. The Americans also left after the United States cut its diplomatic ties with Egypt as a result of our country's intervention in Yemen. But the cutback on programming banished the popular televised soccer games and the broadcast of concerts by a famous Egyptian singer, Om Kalsoum. The loss of these concerts constituted a real cultural deprivation for Egyptians. Arabs would come from all over the Middle East to hear her sing. Her concerts would begin at 8:30 P.M., and when she sang her last words at 4:00 A.M. her audience would still be there. Her voice had such power that more than once she was said to have blown out microphones that could not adapt to her volume.

·

Ezz was called to active duty at an army base eighty miles from Cairo. He had only four days of leave each month. It had been decided that on these days he would visit me in my mother's home. In public his demeanor was fairly even, but in our bedroom the battle continued. He seemed to come to Cairo primed for abuse. I was doing my best not to give Ezz any excuse to beat me. All the same, the psychological pain I endured from him was worse than anything he could have done to me physically.

During the year after I moved to my mother's house Ezz beat me twice. It was hard to keep it a secret. The mistreatment I received became an open issue when Rokaya protested my husband's treatment of me in my mother's home. "Everyone can see that Camelia is at home day and night," she said. "Everyone can see there is no basis for what he is doing." After the first beating in her house my mother called my uncle Taalat and asked for his help. He went to my father. But as usual, Father did nothing. After the second beating, Rokaya confronted my father again, but still he did nothing to protect me. To do so would have gone against the moral code endorsing a man's total mastery over his wife.

I began to realize that I had to do something to help myself. I remembered Ezz throwing me out of the house in the middle of the night. I remembered my father's threat that I would be thrown out of the family when I broached the topic of divorce. What would I do if I had to make my own way? My mind turned to my education. After all, Rawia was now completing her education.

The first time I mentioned the idea to Ezz he rejected it categorically. I decided to try to persuade my father. This was after having avoided him for the better part of 1968. I had moved in with my mother earlier in the year. Father had ordered me not to talk about Ezz with anyone except him—and I believed that was his way of burying the issue and controlling me.

I went to my father's home toward the end of 1968. I had carefully rehearsed what I would say to him. It had become a habit in my conversations with him since I knew he had little time for me and also he was enormously adept at deflecting conversations he did not want to hear. He greeted me cordially. Usually I kissed his hand and we embraced and shared a kiss. This time he was distant. He tried to make small talk. I sensed that he did not want to talk about what he had heard from Rokaya and Uncle Talaat about my affairs.

"How is your daughter?" he inquired. I responded.

"You are looking weak," he commented. I had been on a diet. I deflected further discussion on that topic.

Even before I began my argument about returning to school I believed Father's answer would be yes. The whole family, including my father, considered education very important. I outlined my proposal. "Rawia is going to school, and I want to go with her," I added.

I was becoming angry as I watched my father's stern face. I wondered why he always believed Ezz. Did he really believe I was playing around? He had always treated me like a child, I thought. He did not weigh what I told him but lectured me on my behavior, giving me his interpretation of what was going on. "Did Rokaya tell you what has been happening to me for the past six months?" I suddenly asked, unable to keep my thoughts in.

My parents on their wedding day in November 1940. My father was twenty-three and a second lieutenant in the Egyptian army.

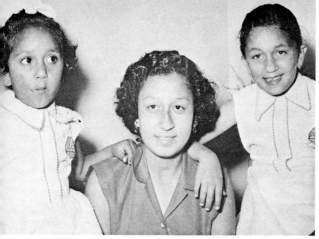

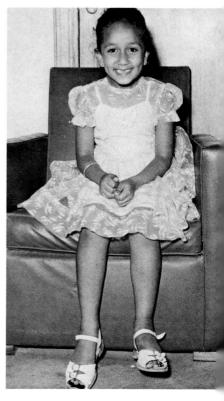

Top left: Aged six, with my sisters Rokaya and Rawia. *Right:* In my father's office at the newspaper *Al-Gumhuriah.*

Talking with President Nasser. My grandfather, Mohammed el-Sadat, looks on. On my father's left is Marshal Abdel Hakim Amer.

Sit el-Barein (Father's mother) with her grandchildren, Rawia, Rokaya, and me (clockwise from left).

Father's relatives. Father with Lobna on his lap. To his right (seated) are his father, his mother, his brother Talaat, and his sister Nafeisa. Standing (left to right) are Father's stepbrother, Rokaya, his stepsister, and brother Esmat. On the floor below Father is Rawia and to her right Father's stepbrother 'Atif.

Mother's relatives. On my father's right is Rokaya's fiancé, Amin, and behind him my mother. Rawia (with glasses) and I are on the floor, and behind me is my cousin and childhood playmate Ibrahim.

Father, Rawia and I with Mohammed Madi, the *omda* of Mit Abul-Kun, in front of El Dawar.

Rawia and I were married in a joint ceremony. (From left to right) Ezz and I, Amin, Rokaya and her son Mohammed, Rawia and Galal.

Rawia and I with Jihan.

Shaking hands with President Nasser.

Left: May 1969. Jihan and Father. (Front from left to right) Noha, Gamal, Lobna, Rawia, Little Jihan, and I. *Right:* July 1972. (Standing from left to right) Noha, little Jihan, Rokaya, Lobna, and I. On the floor are Soha (Rokaya's daughter), Ashraf (Rokaya's son), and Lulee (my daughter).

August 1972. (From right to left) Father, Jihan, Rokaya, Soha, Amin, Gamal, and Mohammed (Rokaya's son).

My mother in 1971. Before going on her pilgrimage to Mecca she wore modern clothes and did not confine her hair.

My mother dressed for her 1972 pilgrimage to Mecca.

Mother in 1976 with Lulee and me and with Lotfa and Rahma, her lifelong friends who had accompanied her when she visited my father in jail during the 1940s.

1972. With 'Atif, Father's young stepbrother, the pilot who was killed a few months later in the October War.

February 1974. I was in Sinai on a business trip when the Egyptian troops started to move in.

"Yes, yes," he said solemnly. "I know. I know."

Though Father was usually warm at the outset of a meeting he often became sharp after he sat down. I was nervous. I was sitting stiffly, looking directly at him. This time my father did not attempt to defend Ezz. It seemed he now wanted to do what he could to please me. I wondered whether he regretted having allowed Ezz to mistreat me for so long.

He cannot look me in the eye, I thought. Usually I was the one who could not meet his gaze. The thought struck me that I had won a victory—perhaps in more ways than one. He feels guilty, I thought. Now there is a chance he will let me return to school.

"If you are sure that you can do it and still take care of your responsibilities," Father finally said, "then I think it would be a good idea."

We got up. This time there was no parting embrace. He did not want to appear to be giving in.

The next time Ezz came home on his monthly leave, I told him of my plans to return to school, with my father's approval. He was frustrated, since he dared not oppose my father's consent. "If I see a book lying around here," he told me, "I am going to rip it into pieces." I just looked at him. What could anyone say to such an irrational declaration? "You are not going to make it," Ezz continued. "I know. You are a child—and stupid." I stood before him as a nineteen-year-old grown woman, but Ezz would always see me as a child.

I began planning to enter a preparatory summer term before beginning the September term. Ezz was still unrelenting. During one of his leaves I failed to put away a book that I had been reading in bed. True to his word, Ezz shredded the book with his hands. I returned to the bedroom and found it, picked up the remains, and said nothing. It was my mistake for having left it there.

This was one of the calmest periods of our marriage. Ezz seemed largely defeated. His behavior seemed to say: No one likes me. No one respects me. Everyone knows about me. Rokaya lost no chance to needle Ezz. "Well, big guy," she would tease, "how many times did you beat your wife today?" Her jibes were in the open, for anyone to hear. When I went with my sisters to my father's home, Ezz no longer wanted to go along.

By this time I had begun to feel that I was gaining power over Ezz, because my family began to rally around me. However, Father's coolness still disturbed me. Why did he not tell me how he felt about Ezz's treatment of me? Even if he had said that he had to take Ezz's side against me, that would have showed me that he really cared.

I increasingly regarded my education as a means of gaining my father's respect. One of the few times during this period that he had seemed enthusiastic about me was when I talked about the type of school I was going to enter. It catered to those who worked, and it granted the equivalent of a junior high school diploma in one year. Father expressed his support, especially when I told him I feared I would not be successful. I had been out of school for a long time and would have to take courses that condensed three years of material. "Camelia," Father said, "I know you. When you want to do something, you always do it. I know you are bright. You only need to develop self-discipline." Afterward he began to advise me on how to make a reading schedule, how to handle other schoolwork and also manage my duties as a housewife.

After I entered school and had been studying Arabic I reported to Father that one teacher had said no one in class knew grammar as well as I did. He congratulated me and said, "I told you that you could do it!"

Father always drove to Mit Abul-Kum for Friday prayers. One day I asked him if I might go with him since I did not have a car of my own. His face lit up. "It will be good to have your company, Camelia, since I always go alone," he said. Our relationship took on a new warmth. Father seemed to be proud of me and, for a while, we became close again.

Not too long after that, Ezz's father, General Gamil Attia Abdelbary, then retired from the army, unexpectedly fell ill.

Ezz's younger brother came to tell me that his father was sick. The elderly retired general seemed to be failing rapidly. Since he received a pension he was not entitled to ambulance service to take him to a military hospital. I called my father, and within a short time four doctors and an ambulance arrived at the Abdelbary home. My father-in-law was moved to a hospital. A week later, he died. It was my father who broke the news to Ezz's mother.

My uncles Talaat and Esmat made the funeral arrangements. Our religion dictates that the funeral be held quickly. Unlike Western society, where funerals serve mainly to dissipate the grief of the survivors, Muslim society holds that the main objective of the funeral is the spiritual well-being of the deceased. For that reason, it was to proceed even though some of General Abdelbary's children were not in Cairo, including Ezz.

My father led the funeral procession. Because he was in the government, various government ministers also attended. President Nasser sent a representative. Ezz and another brother, also in the military, did not arrive until after the services were held. My mother-in-law cornered me in front of others, including my mother, and began to berate me for going back to school. "So, you're going to school?" she shrilled. "What good is that?"

"Your son is away twenty-six days of the month," I ventured. But Hamida Abdelbary nagged on.

"You hope to earn money?" she said. "I can pay you to be a servant for my son."

My mother's eyes caught mine. "Do not dare answer!" they said.

Forty days after the death of a family member, relatives are expected to travel to the burial site, which in this case was the village of General Abdelbary, and take gifts of money, pastry, or fruit.

I was prepared to meet my obligation. I asked my father to arrange a car and driver. I asked Ezz's mother if she wanted to ride to the village in our car. "No, no," she replied. "We are not going." The next day I found that Ezz had disappeared with his clothing. I sent someone to his mother's house to locate him, but he was not there. My mother and I went by car to the village. When we arrived at the burial place everyone was there, including my mother-in-law and Ezz. We were greeted warmly by everyone but them.

Later, Ezz's mother again confronted me about her son. "Do you want him?" she asked provocatively, meaning to take him with her.

"No," I replied quietly but firmly.

Hamida led him away.

That night Ezz packed his clothes and left. I did not ask him why he was packing. I thought perhaps he just needed more clothes at the army base. Also, I wanted no confrontation after the long day in his father's village. When it was time for him to return for his usual four-day stay, he did not appear, however. I learned from his brother that he was staying at his mother's house.

I was not sure why he stayed away. He had hardly shown great sensitivity in the past. I suspected that he did not want to talk about an issue I had raised about our daughter's education. Just before the death of his father I mentioned that I wanted to send Lulee to Cairo's German school, a private institution. Rawia and I had both studied there.

"No," was Ezz's emphatic reply. "No private school! I received my education in public school, and it is a good education. She is not going to any private school."

It was obvious, however, that Ezz cared less about public education than about his wallet. He did not intend to pay for a private school, and he avoided me because he did not wish to hear any more on the subject. He stayed away for six months, and while I was spared further abuse from him, I also did not receive the support he had been providing. I had to ask Father for money.

The separation finally ripened my desire for a divorce. I also brooded with increasing resentment on my father's agreement to my marrying at such a young age and his support of my husband. I had been deeply wounded by Father's lack of sympathy after it was obvious that my marriage had gone disastrously wrong. Other Muslim fathers would have beaten up such a son-in-law and yet my father had taken Ezz's side. My anger had built up over the years until I now knew I had to talk to him about it.

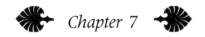

Chapter 7

THE VICE-PRESIDENT
UNDER STRESS

ON DECEMBER 20, 1969, Gamal Abdel Nasser appointed my father vice-president, the first since Egypt became a republic in 1952. The appointment was made at the Cairo airport. Nasser was then in ill health, suffering from high blood pressure, heart disease, and diabetes. Nasser, my father, and Hakim Amer, the military commander in chief, had been close friends. In fact, when my father suffered his first heart attack in the early 1960s, he asked Nasser and Hakim Amer to take care of his children if he should die first. The three of them read the Fatiha, the first sura of the Koran, to seal the pledge that if any of them died first, the remaining members would take care of the family of the deceased. In fact, Hakim Amer would die first and then Nasser, and Father was destined to keep his promise until his death.

In addition to the series of political crises in which my father was involved during the 1960s, he also became entangled in a family matter that precipitated a serious confrontation with Nasser.

After Father became the vice-president Jihan went to visit a rich man. The house enchanted Jihan. Since the host's wife had died and he had no family living with him, Jihan proposed that she buy the house. By this time my father had stipulated that his city house would go to Jihan in the event of his death, so she could use that property to capitalize her proposed purchase. The old man declined her proposal. But it seems Jihan pursued the matter. The old man, who had been an army acquaintance of Nasser's, then wrote him, asking him to help dissuade Jihan from buying the house. Evidently, the man felt he was under some sort of political pressure. Just before Nasser left on one of his secret visits to the Soviet Union in search of military aid to replenish the losses the Egyptian army had sustained in the 1967 war, he handed Father the letter about Jihan.

My stepmother is a strong and independent woman. She would never intentionally do anything to injure my father, but I am not sure she always considered the consequences of her actions. For example, in an interview with the syndicated U.S. columnist Marian Christy, Jihan was once quoted as saying that when my father reproached her for doing something that displeased him, she would reply that since it was in the past, it was not worth discussing. I can see how her attitude might have distressed my father, for he took great pride in his honesty and his public reputation. Jihan's behavior in this case was not only embarrassing for Father but gave his adversaries an opportunity to generate rumors that hurt him. As a result Father came to be regarded as an outsider and a potential threat.

When my father became the Egyptian vice-president, I began to notice changes in both his and Jihan's attitude toward his first family. They became more distant and increasingly inaccessible. In the summer of 1969 Father was living in one of the presidential palaces in a suburb of Cairo. One day he sent my older sister Rokaya, who had her own car, to collect Rawia and myself for a rare visit. I was determined to express some of my feelings to him.

Father was sitting in the second-floor living room when we entered, dressed in blue pajamas and a matching robe. It was evening and the large room was brightly lit. Jihan and Lobna, then eleven years old, were also there.

Father began with the usual greetings. When he got to me, I shot back, sullenly, "How do you think I am?"

We moved out to the darkened balcony, off the living room. I continued to be truculent. "My husband is treating me badly, and it is your fault," I said, my voice gaining volume.

"Why did you have to marry me off at twelve years of age?" I almost shouted. "Did you have to sell me off like a slave? Did I have to be turned out like an animal, to fend for myself in the streets? Did you lack money to feed your daughter, Father?"

My father's eyes flashed. "How dare you shout at me!" he raged. "Out! Out!" he cried, waving his arms. "If you want to shout, then leave the premises." I was thrown out of my father's house.

Two days later dismay suddenly replaced my righteous anger.

Rokaya arrived with the news that Father had suffered a second heart attack.

God! What have I done? I thought, remembering our confrontation. Have I killed my father with my anger? What I did not know was that my father had summoned Rokaya, Rawia, and myself to tell us that he had already suffered a heart attack, and as a result his physician had insisted that he move to his Mit Abul-Kum house in order to reduce the stress he was experiencing.

After learning of his move Rokaya, the only one of us who had a car, had gone daily to the village. She had not told anyone she was going. She returned with the news that Father had refused to use oxygen. When Rawia and I insisted that we should go to our father's side Rokaya objected. I learned that Jihan had told her that we were not wanted because we would cry and make Father nervous. To the devil with that advice, I decided. He is our father, too. Rokaya often acted as though Father were the king and she were the princess. This time she would not stand in our way.

"Neither you nor Jihan has a right to keep us from Father when he is so ill," I told Rokaya sternly. Rawia agreed.

When I returned home that day after learning about Father's illness I found my mother in tears. She, too, had learned about Father's heart attack. Although Mother knew of my problems with Ezz she felt that I should not have burdened my father with accusations about the marriage he had arranged for me.

"How could you talk to your father as you did?" she scolded. "You know he wants the best for you. How was he to know that Ezz would be like this? Go and apologize to your father!" she ordered. Feeling hurt and self-righteous, I refused.

Later, when I left to see my father, Mother implored me to reconsider. "Camelia, be nice to your father. Apologize to him, daughter, because if anything should happen to him—God forbid—then God will never forgive you."

Mother always believed that God's blessings never come to children who do not earn their parents' blessings. She believed that bad things happen to those who mistreat their parents—and she believed I was committing a grave offense against my father.

The next day Rawia and I rented a limousine to take us to Mit Abul-Kum. We felt proud of ourselves because we had never done such a thing by ourselves. We had to borrow money for the limousine and for flowers that we intended to take. The car and driver cost us all of two pounds, but in Cairo at the time, that was enough to feed two people for days.

We directed the driver to a florist shop owned by one of Father's friends. "Give us a dozen of those red ones," Rawia said. Then I said, "No, make it two dozen." The florist worked quickly, and we kept adding to the purchases. If flowers were like a miracle drug, Father surely would be cured almost immediately. With the help of the florist and the driver we stuffed the front seat with blossoms. Finally Rawia and I piled into the back.

When we arrived, Father was not on his deathbed as we had imagined but sleeping on a couch outdoors. I fell to my knees, crying and asking his forgiveness. "Do not be foolish," Father said calmly. His voice was like soothing oil. "I was ill before you came to my house. I was angry because you did not seem to understand that I wanted only happiness for you in arranging your marriage. I would never have sold you for any price or given you to anyone whom I thought would treat you badly."

In some families the father would either have beaten the offending son-in-law or hired others to do a good job of it as a punishment and a warning. But at the sound of these words all critical judgment of my father's behavior during the years of my marriage was suspended.

Father's mind drifted to other things that concerned him. "If your mother ever needs anything, you tell me," he said. "She does not have to know you told me." He asked how Mother was doing. I said she had been having pain since her 1959 surgery and had gone to consult a doctor. He advised her that the surgery would need to be repeated soon or there would be complications.

"And did she go for the operation?" Father asked.

"We are still waiting for a bed in the hospital where my brother-in-law works," I replied. "If she goes to a private doctor it will be very expensive."

Father became agitated. "You leave your mother in pain till you find an empty bed?" he shouted at Rawia and me. "You go immediately and take her to the best doctor. I will pay all the expenses."

When we told him Mother might not agree he instructed us to tell her we were paying. "You must take good care of your mother," he said. "She has no one except you, her children." I reflected on the love they still held for each other.

Later that day Jihan approached Rawia and me. "Do you have a picture of your grandmother?" she asked. "Ever since Anwar has been here he has been wanting a picture of his mother," she continued. "We had one, but I am not sure where it is now." I promised to try to locate a copy of a portrait.

When it was time for us to return to Cairo I learned that Jihan was returning to the city each night, then motoring back to the village to spend the day with Father. This was Father's will. There was a doctor in residence, however. And he wanted us to know that he was keeping watch over Father. "I will be here to take care of him—no need for you to worry," he assured us.

Father was adamant about our not staying. "No, you go home. I will send a car for you when I am better. Then you can come see me." He seemed happy.

It was a good thing the doctor was keeping Father under surveillance, for that night he had another heart attack. The doctor had checked him periodically, but God knows what would have happened if he hadn't been there. Father was a difficult patient. He refused to rest. He refused oxygen. He refused almost all advice. A few days later Father sent a car for us. Uncle Said, who had been visiting us in Cairo, went with us. Ordinarily he would have called to make sure his visit would be received, so when we arrived at the village we went to check with Father.

"I cannot see him," he said. "I do not need more troubles." I do not know whether he meant that Jihan did not want him entertaining one of my mother's brothers, but I suspect that was a possible reason. Father went on in an apparent attempt to clarify his decision. "If I see him, then I would have to see all of the others, too."

Uncle Said was a very sensitive individual—a real softie. He wept when he was told he could not visit Father. In my father's month of recovery in Mit Abul-Kum, neither Uncle Said nor any other member of my mother's family was allowed to visit him. There are only two family events where I can remember them being included.

Rawia's and my wedding in 1962 was one such occasion, and
Rawia's second marriage party, which was to be held in Mit Abul-
Kum in 1974, was another.

•

About six months after Ezz left me, I was approached by Uncle
Esmat, Father's brother, whom Ezz had begged to intervene in our
marital conflict. "Camelia," Uncle Esmat said, "I am bringing Ezz to
see you."

"No," I replied. I did not want to see Ezz, much less live with him
again.

Uncle Esmat began to apply what I call "sweet pressure." "Your
father will not be involved in this," he said. "I will be the guarantor
of your happiness. You can dictate the terms and I will see to them."

By this time I really did not want him back. But Uncle Esmat was
so persistent and persuasive that it was hard to resist his appeal.

"After talking to him," he said, "I do not see the problem."

"He beats me, abuses me, and then runs away," I summed up.
"He is irresponsible."

"Well," said Uncle Esmat with a shrug, "we do not want to upset
your father. He has problems enough."

"The day that Ezz touches you," reassured Uncle Esmat, "is the
day that I get you the divorce. There will be no question of his
running to your father then. He said he admits what he has done to
you, but he does not know why he did it. He says if you take him
back he will do better." I gave in.

Ezz began returning to my mother's home on leave from the
Second Army encampment. Even my mother urged me to try to
make a go of the marriage. "He has admitted he was wrong," she
reminded me. We lived together for a year—well, at least for the four
days each month when he came back from the encampment. Ezz
was a lot quieter and was on his best behavior. That is, there were no
confrontations. I was cool but correct.

•

In September 1970, President Nasser died at age fifty-two. After
Egypt's defeat in the Six-Day War his health deteriorated rapidly. In
1967, he was afflicted by severe diabetes. Then, in September 1969,
he suffered a heart attack. A year later, he suffered a fatal heart
attack. His physicians lost a two-hour struggle to save him.

The news stunned us all. I remember the moment I learned of it. I was sitting with Ezz at the Officers' Club, a new place built only three months earlier on the bank of the Nile River. Suddenly the street behind the club was full of people running and screaming. Then the people at the table next to ours ran to the street. "Ezz, go see what is going on," I urged. He refused.

I saw a man I knew as Soroor, who was in charge of the club's parking lot. He had served as a private aide to President Nasser during the 1948 war. The war cost Soroor an arm. Nasser got the Officers' Club job for him. "What is happening?" I asked.

"It is God's will, ma'am," he replied. Then he turned to Ezz and said, "I think you had better take your wife home now."

We then learned of the death of the apparently indestructible Gamal Abdel Nasser. Although it was not clear then, my father was to be thrust into the role of the acting president of Egypt. It fell to Father to formally announce Nasser's death. The state funeral would be held in three days, he said.

At Mother's house that night things were exceptionally solemn. My sister Rokaya came with her children to stay over. Her husband, a major, had been called up when a state of emergency was declared on the night of Nasser's death. Ezz was to report the next day.

All of the children were put up in one room. Ezz was in my room, and Rokaya, Rawia, and I would stay in Mother's room with her. The silence outside was broken from time to time by the cries and laments of Egyptians who were passing in the street. Many carried Nasser's picture. I thought Ezz seemed detached or preoccupied. He went back and forth between the bedroom and the refrigerator. I caught glimpses of him munching pears.

Mother, my sisters, and I could not decide what we should do about Nasser's funeral. Should we ask Father or should we just go? "It is a family obligation to attend," Mother counseled. "Your father will not have time now to be telling individuals in the family what their own obligations are. As for myself, I do not plan to go because it might embarrass your father."

Rokaya called one of Nasser's family and asked if they were ready to receive visitors. She was told Nasser's home was open to those who wished to offer condolences. We decided to go. Women dressed in black packed the large reception hall in the Nasser home. Fur-

niture divided the area into four areas. The reception hall opened
onto an oblong room. There were other seating arrangements that
were even bigger. We found Nasser's wife, Tahia, sitting on a sofa.
She was surrounded by family members and ministers' wives whom
we knew. Her daughters sat with others.

As Mrs. Nasser stood to greet us, one of the ladies seated nearby
inquired, "Do you know who they are?"

"Of course," Mrs. Nasser said. "They are Rokaya, Rawia, and
Camelia—Anwar's daughters."

The three of us sat on a sofa next to Nasser's relative Tawhida,
whom we had met previously. Tawhida was the wife of Nasser's
uncle, who had died a year earlier. Small and with thick eyeglasses,
she wore a veil, for she was still in mourning. A while later Jihan
entered. After greeting Mrs. Nasser and the others, but not us, she
sat down next to Nasser's wife. Then she turned her head and
looked at us. She seemed agitated. I thought it was because we had
arrived before she did. She did not talk to us at all. It was as though
she were trying to tell everyone she did not know us. We had heard
from others that when people asked her about her relationship with
us, the first three children of her husband, she would say, "I do not
know them that well."

Later that night I went to Rokaya's house to spend the night
because Ezz was going on duty. The phone rang at eleven o'clock,
and Rokaya answered. It was Jihan. "How dare you take your
mother to Nasser's house?" she snapped. "Are you not aware that
was embarrassing to me?" Her voice was so loud that I could hear it
clearly even though I was at the opposite end of Rokaya's living
room.

Rokaya's reply crackled with electric tension. "First, Nasser's
house is our uncle's house—and the nation's, as well. Everybody can
go. Second, who told you Mother was there?"

"I saw her sitting next to you, with her glasses and black veil,"
Jihan responded.

Rokaya's voice assumed a sarcastic quality. "Perhaps you'd better
change your glasses. Mother does not wear either glasses or a veil."
Of course it was Nasser's aunt, Tawhida, whom she had seen sitting
beside us.

"Well . . . ," said Jihan, "when I told Anwar he said I had better take this up with you. I did not think you would do anything to embarrass me. But Rawia and Camelia . . . they are just kids."

"I will call Father and explain it to him," Rokaya responded. However, when she tried, Father's secretary told her that he had retired and was not accepting any calls.

After this encounter with Jihan the three of us were left in a quandary as to whether we should attend Nasser's funeral. Should both of Sadat's families be represented? Would Father want the members of both families in one place at one time? My sisters and I became angry at the way we were being treated. But Mother counseled, "Be calm. Do not make yourselves crazy. Your father will explain about all of this when you see him."

We did not see Father. Neither did we get word from him. Eventually we learned that he had ordered an aide not to inform us that we were expected. At the funeral there would be three chairs for us but they would remain vacant.

Nasser's funeral was the grandest one that had been held in the Middle East until that time. Three days were allowed for visiting heads of state and delegations to arrive for the state funeral. Egyptians mourned his death for three days. Mother lived in downtown Cairo, and people could be seen wandering in the streets crying Nasser's name. "Good-bye, Nasser," they wailed. "Good-bye, our leader!"

Nasser's name had become synonymous with Egypt's pride and future, in part because he was the first leader of the country in four hundred years who was a native son and not imposed by some foreign nation. Moreover, he was an Egyptian who stood up to the giants of regional and world politics. When King Saud expressed anger over Nasser's political foray into Yemen, Nasser vowed publicly, "I will pluck out his beard!" When the United States tried to coerce Nasser into pulling out of Yemen, he crowed, "If the United States does not want to drink from the Mediterranean, let them drink the Red Sea."

This popular allegiance to Nasser did not necessarily mean that his policies were successful. Cairo was packed. The flood of evacuees caused the city's population to expand threefold, resulting in a major housing shortage that forced them to invade empty dwellings. The army and the evacuation of zones near the Suez Canal brought about a shortage of food, and without the revenue from the canal there was no money to enable the Nasser government to offset the losses with purchases abroad. Yet, Nasser had maintained his devoted following. People trusted him. He appealed to deeply rooted feelings of nationalism. When he spoke on "The Arab Voice," broadcast by Cairo Radio, the whole Arab world paused to listen.

Nasser's funeral procession was to begin at the headquarters of the Arab Socialist Union. His casket would be transported on a horse-drawn caisson, a two-wheeled wagon used to move ammunition. The mourners, including Egyptian and foreign dignitaries, would walk in the procession as it moved three miles along the Nile River to the Free Officers' building, where the revolution had been announced. From there, the casket and official mourners were to be transported by motor vehicles to a mosque in Heliopolis, a Cairo suburb twelve miles away, where Nasser's body would be entombed.

That was the plan, but Nasser's emotional followers forced a change. They did not want a caisson to carry the casket. They wanted to pay Nasser homage by carrying his casket the entire distance. In Egypt, mourners sometimes show their devotion to the deceased by sharing in the carrying of the casket. Different pallbearers exchange positions and take up the load as the procession moves on. In this case the crowds went wild as thousands of hands reached toward the Egyptian leader's casket.

Soon an army helicopter had maneuvered over the scene, the downthrust of its blades whirling dust into the air. Officials cleared a landing site, then forced a pathway through the throng of mourners and put Nasser's casket into the helicopter. The propellers began to beat out a quickened cadence, and the helicopter lifted off en route to the mosque in Heliopolis. I watched the funeral on TV. Coverage depicted scenes throughout Cairo. People climbed lampposts and trees, hoping for a glimpse of the funeral procession. Balconies were packed with curious onlookers. That day Cairo was a sea of people. It is a scene I will never forget.

My father and the other mourners began the three-mile procession to the Free Officers' headquarters. During the walk Father collapsed. It was only three weeks since his previous heart attack. He was carried to the Free Officers' building, where he received medical attention, and was back on his feet within a half hour, we learned later. He went on to the mosque by car to attend Nasser's last rites.

On the night of Nasser's funeral his home was open to those who wished to visit the family. Rokaya, Rawia, and I went together. Jihan, who was also there, still did not talk to us.

Only the next day, by reading newspapers and watching TV, did we learn the details of Nasser's funeral and of Father's collapse.

•

Father was ordered to rest after his collapse, one newspaper reported. The second day Rokaya tried to reach him by phone but was told that he had been moved from the house where he had been staying. Two days later, Rokaya said she had learned where Father was staying but could not reach him by phone. Worried, we decided we should go to him. When we arrived security guards at the entry would not admit us even when we explained that we were Sadat's daughters. They sent to ask my stepsisters if we were indeed related. Even now it is difficult to explain how much that hurt.

After spending an hour with our stepsisters, Rokaya, Rawia, and I were told that Father awaited us in a room on the main floor. A bed had been set up there so that he would not have to climb the stairs. Rokaya led the way into his room.

"What are you doing here?" he asked. Rokaya was so taken aback that she mumbled incoherently. Rawia just said hello. I was the last to speak. "We were so worried from the little news we got that we thought we should come. Rokaya tried to reach you by phone but could not. So, here we are," I said. We were not thinking about how Father had been treating us. We were really sad.

Father stared. When he spoke his voice seemed angry. "You should not believe everything you hear. If I want you, I will send for you," he said.

Jihan was sitting on the bed next to my father. She was cordial, but it did not help to dispel the tension that was so palpable. We left about twenty minutes later.

It now seems clear to me that Father wanted his peace of mind at home. Keeping Jihan and Rokaya separated was one way of ensuring that tranquillity. I think he banked on the realization that whatever he did, his first wife and her three daughters would not reject him, no matter what their feelings were. We, his children, were brought up under traditions that teach that individuals are good only to the extent that they are loyal to their parents, and especially their father.

Father, I think, also believed that if the public became aware that he had conflict in his family life and could not manage it, they would not trust him to run a country torn by conflict. Nasser's death marked the end of one era and the beginning of another. Father desperately needed the trust and support of the Egyptian people as a result of this latest national crisis that thrust him into the presidency. After an interim period, during which his control of the government might be endangered by major challenges, he had to face a national election to affirm his presidency.

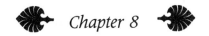

Chapter 8

MY FATHER, MY PRESIDENT

THREE MONTHS after Nasser's death, the presidential elections were held in December 1970. The newspapers reported that Sadat would vote at the primary school in Mit Abul-Kum and would await the election results in his home in the village. Uncle Fat-hy called that day to ask when we would arrive in the village. The whole village would be celebrating, he said. The preparations on behalf of my father's anticipated victory were really impressive, he reported.

We three daughters of his first marriage did not go. We feared that we were not welcome, since Father had said he would call us if he wanted us. He had not called. We could envision the guards turning us away, especially after having been shut out by them the previous time, even though we had identified ourselves as his daughters.

The next day newspapers headlined a first interview with the new president. When asked by reporters about his family, Father mentioned only Jihan and their children. We first three children of Anwar el-Sadat were evidently to become nonpersons. Could our father be so callous toward us?

We also learned through Rokaya, who had a friend in the Ministry of Foreign Affairs, that when Father was asked to list on his official protocol the names of family members to be invited to events, his first three daughters were omitted. That was a severe blow. The omission in the news interview could have been unintentional or an error of reporting, but this latest affront clearly reflected Father's personal position.

What had we done wrong? we wondered. Were we not presentable? Rokaya, as the oldest and the one who used to represent us to him in our problems, said she would call Father. Rokaya had a big-sister mentality since Father had said he always relied upon her wisdom to teach her younger sisters and take care of them.

She called Father that night and said she wanted to discuss with him, face-to-face, an important family matter.

"I am very busy," he replied. "I will call you when I am free." Obviously Father knew why she wanted to talk to him and did not return her call until after his election party in Mit Abul-Kum.

We learned that after his victory was confirmed he had a big party and that all of his family and relatives attended—except us, because we were not invited. Rokaya, who treasured her position as her father's firstborn, wanted to talk to him about our situation but was so heartsick that she could not bring herself to approach him. Why is he doing this to us? we all wondered. But we never found an answer. I even asked my mother, and she, who always had a defense for her former husband, could not find words to defend him.

Apart from the fact that Rawia and I became celebrities in the school for housewives that we were attending, we were in a calm backwater, away from Cairo's political currents. The two of us continued to use public transportation to go to school. Rawia was twenty-four and I was twenty-one. We could imagine ourselves arriving at the home of the president of Egypt on a bus only to be turned away by the guards. Rawia and I had become sensitive about possible future rejections. Meanwhile, Rokaya kept trying to get back into Father's life. She called and went to his house. Unlike Rawia and me, Rokaya did not mind arguing with anyone, including the guards at Father's home. But in a very real sense we three daughters of Father's first marriage were relegated to the status of outsiders, though he continued to give Rawia five Egyptian pounds a month for support as his divorced daughter. Ezz contributed three pounds a month to my upkeep—about enough for cigarettes.

•

Two more months passed, and all that we knew about our father's life was gleaned from newspapers. Politically, we were well informed. Personally, we knew nothing. It was sad, even depressing, this new relationship.

Father was busy during this time. There were daily interviews in the press with the new president. He stressed the continuity between his government and Nasser's regime. He used Nasser's name to legitimize his own power. Reading the interviews, one might have come to the conclusion that Father had become merely a caretaker for the memory of Nasser's government. He used the phrase "Nasser, may he rest in peace" so many times in speeches during the early days of his new presidency that it became a national joke. I believe Father had doubts that the Egyptian people would accept him as their leader, since Nasser had been so charismatic. Later, it became evident that Father did have his own political agenda. He wanted to unite the country and build a power base from which he could regain Egypt's land and honor. That meant that he had to find a way to make both the United States and Israel regard him seriously. It would also involve seeking help from the Soviet Union to rebuild the Egyptian army.

Although Father had been identified with the revolutionary movement, people did not know what to expect of him as their new leader. However, his mastery of the government and his popularity grew during his first year in office. One of his first decisive acts, which affected many Egyptians, was to revoke the governmental custodianship over the property of large landowners, initiated during the Nasser regime. When people recognized me on the street as President Sadat's daughter, they would stop me and say, "God bless your father for what he has done."

Father became a hero to many when he ordered the release of those—mostly Muslim Brotherhood members—who had been made political prisoners during the Nasser regime. The personal dimension of the imprisonments became obvious to us, because one of my mother's relatives was among those who were released. He talked about what went on in prison, including being tortured. There had been no safeguards to ensure a speedy trial of the accused—or any trial at all, for that matter. The popular response to the freeing of the political prisoners seemed to me a sure sign that Egyptians were coming to recognize Father as a leader in his own right.

Father also gained a reputation for astuteness and decisiveness in his handling of a plot to depose him and his government in 1971. During that period there was widespread phone tapping at the national level in Egypt. It was so bad that when we talked on the phone and heard mysterious clicks, we would say, "Hi there! How are you? Come on and join in on our conversation." A group known as the Central Power Bloc, consisting of many major Egyptian figures, including government ministers, sought control, contending they were Nasser's true heirs. The military opposed them. One day a police officer who was taping conversations heard of a plot to overthrow Sadat. The discussants reportedly said that if my father attempted to reach a radio station to rally support, he would be assassinated.

The officer tried to contact the president but was unable to. He then went to the husband of one of my aunts. My uncle contacted Father's secretary Fawzi and tried to arrange a meeting "on a matter of great urgency." He refused to identify the topic. Consequently Father's secretary was reluctant to allow him access. My uncle was insistent. Finally, Father accepted the call and spoke to the officer. "Siadet al-Rayes" (the formal address for the president), "I have a tape recording. It is vital that you hear it." Father listened to the tape. Two days later the plotters were arrested. Many people who talked to me about the incident were impressed by Father's retaliation. The fact that he had learned of a planned coup and acted to thwart it was proof of his savvy. Afterward, Father ordered the tapes of the private conversations to be destroyed.

Father shut down detention centers. He also ordered that arbitrary detention of suspects without court review be terminated. Because Egypt was technically in a continuing, declared state of war, the liberalization under my father during his first years in office did not include freedom of the press. It was not until 1974 that he relaxed governmental control over the Egyptian press.

In his book *In Search of Identity* Father gives an idea of the immensity of the problems confronting him:

Our relations with Arab and West European countries, as well as the United States, were in shreds. We had what one could call relations only with the Soviet Union—a country that never made us feel there were advantages in having relations with it, since the Russians had practically no relations with anybody. Added to this were some facts I had found out for myself—facts which confirmed that none of the officials in Nasser's entourage ever paid any regard to the interests of Egypt and wanted nothing but to remain in power, seeking their own interests and motivated by hatred and jealousy. So it was only natural that my spirit of challenge should be even further strengthened. . . . I knew that . . . I should have to challenge many conditions and ethical codes in existence at the time; but I believed I had the capacity for this. . . . And now that I was President, I felt I wielded a tremendous *real* power, which had to be used in doing good.

Despite my personal frustration at his inaccessibility, I began to love my father in his new role as my president—even if at a distance—because of the way I saw him through the eyes of my countrymen.

One day one of Father's secretaries called Rokaya's home with the news that "the president is expecting the three of you next week." The fact that it was a secretary and not Father who called made us even more nervous.

When the time came, we had all dressed carefully. We were ready to meet our father, and our president. We went in Rokaya's car. Once again, when we arrived the guards blocked us until they could verify that we were President Sadat's daughters. Being kept out of Father's home was as offensive as if strangers had denied me access to my own home. It seemed that with each visit the guards would have to be convinced that we existed.

The house we went to was one Father had bought a year earlier. It was still in the hands of the decorators. The house had a Nile River view, but the building was much smaller than the house on Pyramids Avenue. Eventually someone came to accompany us past the guards. We did not know him.

We were ushered into a waiting room, where we were delayed a few minutes more. Then Father entered, followed by Jihan, my stepsisters Lobna, Noha, and Nana (little Jihan), and my stepbrother, Gamal. Father and Jihan were in good spirits, talking about their new life and how people were discussing them. I decided to join in.

Father always enjoyed jokes, including political ones. Many of the political jokes in Egypt center on the president and the government. Sometimes they are funny. Sometimes they are intended as criticism. Some of the jokes are intertwined with rumor, which is one form of daily news in Egypt.

I told Father about a rumor that he had married a young girl and kept her in a house in the Cairo suburbs. "I defended you and said you had been married to only Mother and Jihan," I said. "Then the woman who told me this bet me one hundred Egyptian pounds that she could show me the house."

"Why did you not go with her?" Father asked. "You could have made a hundred pounds, Camelia."

"I was afraid I might lose the bet," I quipped.

Everybody started laughing. Father was quick with a comeback. "What would you do if one day, when I die, you find a lady coming to the funeral with two children and she claims that she is the one who was my secret wife?" In Egyptian movies such plots are common. It is accepted that a Muslim man can have more than one wife. Some of them hide the second one, and when the man dies those who are the acknowledged family are astounded when a second bereaved family appears to weep at the funeral—"Oh! My beloved husband! The father of my children!"

Everyone was amused, except Jihan. Her face changed and she spoke in a sharp voice. "I swear to God, Anwar, I would take your body out of the grave and throw it into the Nile," she said, pointing toward the terrace and the Nile River.

I used to think jealousy was a weakness, but I later learned that I, too, could be jealous and remembered the story of A-isha, one of the wives of Mohammed the Prophet. She was known for her wisdom and knowledge, yet she was so jealous that the Prophet had to leave home. No Muslim woman could be better than the Prophet's wife, I thought.

When tea was served I thought I would lighten the atmosphere. "Siadet el-Rayes," I said in a formal manner, "your birthday is next week. Are we allowed to come and say happy birthday or must we fill in an application first?" It seemed a funny thing to say at the time, but now I think I intended to needle him.

Father turned his face to me with a big smile, ready to answer. But Jihan beat him to it. "Of course you have to seek permission first," she said. "Yes. . . . It is the president's house now."

A silence fell over the room. It seemed the joke was no joke. Then a guard entered with a paper for my father to examine. Father's eyes were still scanning the paper when he spoke to me. "Camelia, what day of the week is my birthday?"

"It is next Friday," I answered.

"We will call you," he said in a royal manner "and let you know if we can see you." He had never referred to himself as "we" before.

On the way out of my father's home my sisters and I looked at one another, not saying a word. When we discussed the situation with Mother she said, "Well, your father never celebrated his birthday. Why do you expect him to make a big thing of it now?" That did not end the matter, though. Rawia and I were upset because we just wanted to be with him and make him happy. We did not want to interrupt his life. We got no call inviting us to share his birthday. Feeling hurt, the day of his birthday we decided to go to Mit Abul-Kum very early, reasoning that if he did call, we would not be home.

However, I asked Rokaya if she would join Rawia and me in sending flowers to Father. She suggested that we also send a card with the message, "Your three flowers, Rokaya, Rawia, and Camelia."

Rokaya was the only one of us who actually attended Father's birthday. When he eventually called for Rawia and me, he was told that we were in Mit Abul-Kum for the day. When we saw Rokaya that night she said that at the party Father roared with laughter when he saw her entering. "You really know how to get to her," he said, meaning that Jihan had reacted to our card. "Your flowers were the first to arrive. The servant handed the card to Jihan, who was beside me in bed," he told Rokaya. "The minute she read your 'three flowers' card she exclaimed, 'What! If they are "your flowers," then what would I be?' "

•

One night in 1971 Ezz had just come back from the Second Army camp. He told me that my father, who was then in charge of the military, had visited the front and told the military leaders that if Israel attacked again, they were to abandon their positions and run toward Cairo as quickly as possible. "That does not seem logical," I replied. "As the leader of the military, why would he say that?"

In the 1967 war, when the Israeli troops attacked en masse, Egyptian troops in the Sinai Desert did break and run—an understandable human reaction to apparently overpowering odds. Even the Egyptians scoffed at those who had retreated and called them the "Running Army." It was unthinkable to me that my father, the chief of the Egyptian military, would actually instruct troops to run in the face of an attack. In reality, Egypt was determined to stand its ground against the Israelis, no matter what the cost.

"You do not believe that?" Ezz bellowed. "You . . . you stupid, silly girl! Because you study your stupid, silly books, you think you know everything?"

I stood my own ground, but I was determined not to fight with Ezz, especially in my mother's home. "Well, it just does not seem to me that my father would do that." I was prepared to drop it. But Ezz was not.

"Nadia, our maid, is from the village. But she is smarter than you are now and smarter than you ever will be," he shouted. It was obvious that Ezz was losing control of himself. It was also obvious that this was a crisis point for both of us. He no doubt believed that if he lost I would become increasingly uncontrollable. Increased self-control for me would threaten his traditional dominance as a man. For me, losing would mean that my life and that of my daughter would be under his thumb always. Intellectual, psychological, economic, and physical servitude would be the rule and the norm.

Ezz began to slap and hit me. I retaliated with blows and verbal abuse. Words spewed out of my mouth, words as offensive as those he had used to demean me. Ezz got even madder as I stood against him and screamed my defiance. "Hit me! Hit me!" I shouted. "You can kill me, but you will never bully me again. I am through with you. Do not touch me!"

"You cannot resist me," Ezz said sternly. "I am your husband and your master. I have my rights."

In my own mind I reassured myself that while he could use and abuse my body, he could never control my mind or my soul. There was no way he could rule over me again. The last psychological link that had held us together broke that night.

The next day there was a strained atmosphere in my mother's household. It seemed obvious that what had happened between Ezz and me behind the closed door of our bedroom had gone far beyond the accepted limits. I had to talk to my father on this day in October 1971. He was the one who had imposed such a severe ultimatum when I had first suggested I wanted a divorce. Challenging my father was another test of my growing personal strength and determination. My husband was thirty-eight years old. I was twenty-one, with a five-year-old daughter, yet I still dreaded what might happen. But Father's reaction surprised me.

"So, you want to be divorced," he said. It was not so much a question as an affirmation. I think the reports he had received over the years from Rokaya and other members of the family had had a cumulative effect. Father expressed no disbelief or defiance this time, nor did he reject divorce. Father, as I have said before, was Muslim to his very core, but he was humane and a realist. What was not workable, he recognized. And what was hurting a member of his family, he acknowledged, albeit grudgingly.

Under Islamic law a Muslim male can initiate a divorce against his wife by saying three times, "I divorce thee." However, women's rights in Egypt had long ago reached the point where a woman with good cause could divorce her husband. And that was what I intended to do.

"I do not want anything from Ezz," I declared, "except my daughter, Lulee." All of the ties to Ezz Abdelbary that could be severed were to be cut. Trusting in the support of my father, my mother, my sisters, and the other members of my family, I determined to turn away from Ezz Abdelbary and begin a new life.

Father had promised me quick action on my divorce, and he was in a position to deliver it. But as the days rolled on with no action taken on the matter, I became more and more concerned.

I phoned him at home, but invariably some aide answered with "The president is busy now" or "Mr. President is in a meeting and cannot be interrupted." I explained that I was his daughter, calling on a personal matter, and asked to have my call returned. It never was.

As I went on stewing about my father and my promised divorce, I could not sleep. I would be up day and night for three days at a time. When I finally collapsed from exhaustion, sleep was fitful. Father does not care about me, I told myself. He promised and then broke his promise. Now he does not want me divorced. In my mind I could hear Jihan saying, "You cannot get divorced until Rawia is married again. Your father cannot afford to support two divorced daughters." And so it went through the nights and days.

By the end of 1971 I could not eat. My weight began to drop continuously, from 149 pounds to 103. I was twenty-one years old and looked as though I were on my way to becoming as thin as a toothpick. I turned to Rokaya. "Have you heard anything from Father about my divorce?" I asked.

As the eldest sister, Rokaya was often a conduit of information from Father about his thoughts concerning his younger daughters. Also, if Rokaya wanted information she was not above bullying secretaries and aides until she got through to Father and obtained what she sought. But she had no news either.

I cannot count on anyone, I thought. No one. I am alone. Why is this happening to me? Why does no one help me? After about six weeks of this, I began to get weaker. I threw up repeatedly. Then I began to vomit blood. At that point the family decided to call a doctor. The physician sent me to the Maadi Military Hospital in a Cairo suburb near the Nile. At the time it was the best staffed and equipped hospital in Egypt. I had had a nervous breakdown, they decided. I also had an ulcer, which accounted for the bleeding. I was put on periodic doses of tranquilizers and given an ulcer diet—virtually baby food. Usually I had no desire to eat even gourmet food, so the ulcer diet provided absolutely no motivation to eat.

I rarely got out of bed, I was so weak. But my mind did not let up. I was mad at everyone. No one would intercede with Father. Not even my mother, my most stalwart supporter. I did not stop to consider that as his ex-wife she did not exactly have his favor. I refused to see my mother. I refused to see Rawia, with whom I was especially close. I refused to see Rokaya. I even refused to see my daughter, Lulee. I had decided that no one gave a damn about me. Flowers arrived from my father, but he never even bothered to sign the get-well cards. It was probably the writing of a secretary or presidential aide, I sighed.

After I had been in the hospital for three weeks my father and Jihan arrived. Father was sweet that day, but at the time I was in no mood to have anything to do with him. "Camelia," he said softly, "why are you doing this to yourself? You are always the one show-ing teeth, with smiles for everyone."

I stared at him noncommittally. He tried again. "Camelia, I can stand almost anything, but I cannot stand it if one of my children becomes ill. I can stand up to the Americans, even, but I cannot tell you how helpless I feel when my children are sick."

I just stared at him. "Be well now," Father added. "You must help yourself. You cannot give up. You must not give up."

Angry as I was, I could sense his concern. He was pulling up feelings from deep inside. "I do not know what has happened to you," he said sadly.

"You know well what happened to me," I told him as forcefully as I could. In that comment I thought that I had telescoped and conveyed all the misery I felt I had suffered under his hand or through his indifference. The visit came to an end.

Five weeks after I had been hospitalized, I got a call from the security guards. They said there was a man to see me. When they mentioned his name, Sayed Joda, I recognized it was my hairdresser. When he came up he said, "Well, I have not seen you in a long time. Then I heard you were sick. So I decided to come see you and style your hair. Maybe it will help you get well faster." He brought a kit with the tools of his trade. When he gave me a mirror the face that looked back at me was shocking. I recognized the hairstyle, but the face was pale and drawn. Could I really look that bad? It was time to do something about my life, I decided. Two days later I went to see the chief of the hospital, a friend who had visited me regularly and had tried to cheer me with conversation and jokes. "I am leaving," I told him. "No more drugs. I am going to be fine."

I went back to school, trying to catch up with my senior year. The exams for the whole year were coming up, and I had only a month in which to prepare. The tests were an ordeal. There are comprehensive exams for all subjects, two to three per day for five days. Unfortunately, I failed. To make matters worse, things were not well between my mother and me. She was angry because I had not allowed her to visit me at the hospital. Neither were things well between Rawia and me. She interpreted my refusal to let her visit me as a personal affront, as though I had not wanted to talk to her, of all people.

I began dwelling on the idea that my father owed me help with my divorce. I went to Rokaya. "I need to talk with Father," I implored. She arranged for me to meet with him at her home. When Father and I met, I began to cry. "You do not care, leaving me to hang like this," I said accusingly.

"No one told me that you were trying to contact me," he said earnestly. "I did not know you were in such a rush for a divorce." Father tried to calm me. There were plenty of promises, but no word about action.

Meanwhile, Ezz caused more stress in my life. When I tried to reclaim my possessions—things my father had given me—Ezz threatened me and ordered me to stay away from the house. "I will break your neck if I catch you here again," he said. I believed him. I reported the threat to my father, but there was no reaction. That seemed to confirm to me that he was siding with Ezz. God, what must I endure? I asked myself. Will this period of madness ever end? Why am I being punished? Will life ever be normal again? Day and night, my mind was in turmoil.

Ezz began calling every day. "I am going to bring you home," he said. "You cannot resist me. You are my wife. Your place is in my household." The tension kept building. I felt like a pressure cooker whose escape valve had stuck. It was just a matter of time.

No one talked to me. Everyone seemed angry with me. I did not talk to anyone. The pressure kept building. A month later I was rushed to the hospital in an ambulance. I had tried to kill myself with an overdose of aspirin. Typically, it was not my father who came or called but his secretary, calling on his behalf. He was a short dumpling of a man, one of the sweetest human beings on my father's staff. "The president is hoping that you will be fine," he said, not allowing himself the familiarity of saying, "Your father wishes you well." "He will do whatever you wish," the aide said. "He looks forward to your returning home and continuing your studies. . . ." My eyes and mind registered that his mouth continued to move, but all I heard was "Blah, blah, blah. . . ."

I was in the hospital for three or four days before I returned home. In less than a week after my release from the hospital I received my divorce papers. A presidential secretary showed up with Ezz in tow. I later learned that he had been picked up by two military officers who informed him, evidently on my father's authority, that I wanted a divorce. At that point he did not have much choice.

I signed the forms. The actual divorce came as an anticlimax. After the years of humiliation and suffering I had gone through, I had almost completely relinquished hope that I would ever be able to put my life in order. My breakdown had left me numbed. I felt nothing in regard to my own situation. I experienced no sense of victory or fulfillment. I felt about the same as I would upon signing a check to pay a bill. Neither did I feel anything for anyone else, including my father. His intervention came so late that I could not feel any gratitude toward him.

A day later the secretary went with me to meet Ezz at our home and pick up my possessions. On July 11, 1972, I finally became a divorced woman. I was twenty-two years old. Lulee was six by this time, and Ezz was thirty-nine.

Rawia and I traded statuses: she became engaged. She also quit her job, which she had held with a German firm. She asked me to go to her office to collect the bonus that was owed her. I talked to her boss and he offered me Rawia's old job. While working I again prepared for the high school exams.

I felt liberated. For the first time my life was in my own hands, not my father's, nor my husband's, and I gloried in it. I felt I had survived the long journey that had changed me from a headstrong child into an independent woman and mother. I had eventually managed to express my anger to my father and felt that he had understood it.

A year later I was able to reconcile my feelings toward Ezz. I had never really hated him, but I had hated the abuse. My mother, who can forgive anyone, spoke firmly to me. "Don't think that you can get rid of Ezz simply by divorcing him," she said. "There will always be that bond between you both—your baby, Lulee. You must maintain a relationship with him and his family so that Lulee will know her family. I did the same thing for my children. And, for your own sake, you must truly forgive, Camelia. You are not the sort of person who can live with hard feelings." So, after a year, I visited Hamida with Lulee, and throughout the years I have regularly seen her. Recently, I went to her house. It was the prophet Mohammed's birthday, and *hallawet al mawlid* (candy of the birth) is made specially for the occasion. Hamida was delighted to see me. She talked of Ezz and his second wife and told me how she wanted to arrange for him to remarry me. Thirteen years has certainly been ample time to heal my wounds, and I smiled at the irony of Hamida's professed change of heart.

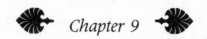 *Chapter 9*

A CONFRONTATION WITH FATHER

FROM THE FIRST DAYS of his presidency my father began analyzing how he could regain the Egyptian territory that was lost to Egypt in the Six-Day War. He also wanted to restore Egypt's self-confidence. In a bold attempt to deal with the problem, Father announced a new "initiative" in the Egyptian parliament on February 4, 1971. The gist was that if Israel would withdraw her forces in Sinai, Egypt would reopen the Suez Canal, move the Egyptian army to the East Bank, extend the Rogers Plan cease-fire (of U.S. Secretary of State William Rogers) by six months, make an official declaration of the cease-fire, restore diplomatic relations with the United States, and sign a peace agreement with Israel under the aegis of the U.N. secretary-general.

Looking back on that initiative, Father wrote in *In Search of Identity*, "If the United States or Israel had shown enough interest in that Initiative, the October War [or Yom Kippur War, which would begin on October 6, 1973] would not have taken place and the process of negotiating peace would have started in February or March 1971."

The United States did not take Father seriously. William Rogers, the U.S. secretary of state, tried to shift the burden of blame onto him, saying he wasted 1971 without moving toward a solution of Egypt's problems with Israel. Further, Rogers pledged that the United States would maintain Israel's military superiority over not only Egypt but all the combined Arab states.

The United States also regarded Egypt as a client of the Soviet Union. However, in reality the Soviets were of virtually no help to Father's government. Pro-Soviet Egyptians were a threat to his presidency. Also, Communists in the neighboring nation of the Sudan attempted a coup but were defeated. As for military support to replace the losses of the Six-Day War or strengthen the Egyptian military, the Soviets repeatedly made promises but delivered little.

110

When the Soviets seemed on the verge of providing equipment, they wanted to have a veto over its use. Father believed that that implied an infringement on Egyptian sovereignty. On July 6, 1972, the Soviets presented him with an analysis that evaded discussion of the promised weapons but stated that the U.S.S.R. believed Egypt would be unable to initiate a war. At the Nixon-Brezhnev summit the Middle East was hardly mentioned despite prior assurances. Father had lost faith in the Soviet Union, which was giving neither arms nor diplomatic priority to Egypt. Father expelled some fifteen thousand Soviet experts. They withdrew, taking with them Egypt's four MIG-25 planes and an electronic warfare broadcast jamming system.

Then, in February 1973, Hafiz Ismail, the Egyptian national security adviser, met with Henry Kissinger in Paris. "The drift of what Kissinger said to Ismail," Father later wrote in *In Search of Identity*, "was that the United States regrettably could do nothing to help so long as we were the defeated party and Israel maintained her superiority"—an ironic situation since the United States was the guarantor of Israel's military supremacy.

Father began preparing for a war. I remember that during this period Rawia and I were invited to view films at Father's home on a couple of occasions. War movies held a fascination for him. At the time we knew nothing about his plans for a new war with Israel to redress the imbalance of power. Father especially showed interest in scenes in which World War II army engineers laid down temporary bridges to facilitate river crossings. Now, it is clear that he sought to understand how Egypt might move its troops across the Suez Canal quickly.

About two weeks prior to the beginning of the new war, Father went to Mit Abul-Kum. He always spent time there when he confronted major decisions, and he invited Rawia and me to the village to be with him. He expressed preoccupation about our household provisions. "Do you have groceries?" he asked. At the time, it seemed an odd question. He went on, "You have sugar, tea, oil . . . things like that? I want you to build up your supplies of food." Father told one of his secretaries to give Rawia and me money to buy food. What we did not know was that his advisers had told him that in the event of a war, food—particularly sugar, rice, oil, and beans—would be in short supply within days after the battle began.

On October 5, 1973, the Soviets, with Egyptian permission, brought in four huge transport planes to evacuate the remaining Soviet citizens from Egypt. To Father this was another demonstration of the Soviets' lack of faith in his regime's ability to defend Egyptian cities. A new war with Israel was just a day away, timed to coincide with the Jewish celebration of Yom Kippur.

At 2:00 P.M. on October 6, 1973, Egypt launched 222 supersonic jets across the Suez Canal. The first wave completed its mission in twenty minutes. Much to Father's sorrow, his youngest stepbrother, 'Atif, a pilot, died within the first minutes of the war. The sudden, effective strike had the intended impact. Father wrote in *In Search of Identity*:

With this admirable air strike, the Egyptian Air Force recovered all it had lost in the 1956 War and the 1967 defeat, and paved the way for our armed forces subsequently to achieve that victory which restored the self-confidence of our armed forces, our people, and our Arab nation. It also restored the world's confidence in us, and exploded forever the myth of an invincible Israel.

Israeli propagandists had boasted that their country's military would "crush the bones of the Egyptians," but the war did not fulfill that prophecy. The Soviets tried to intervene and arrange a cease-fire. U.S. military surveillance showed Israel taking a pounding from the supposedly ineffective Egyptians. Henry Kissinger, seeing Israel's danger, consulted with the Soviet Union to try to obtain a cease-fire. Irate, my father contacted Britain's prime minister Edward Heath and told him to inform Kissinger—since Egypt and the United States had broken off diplomatic relations—that anyone who wanted to discuss a cease-fire would have to negotiate directly with the Cairo government. Father also told the British ambassador in Cairo that there could be a cease-fire if Israel withdrew from the occupied Arab lands.

The United States had been monitoring the war via satellite. Things were going so badly for Israel that, as Father wrote in *In Search of Identity*:

. . . now two American rockets were fired at two Egyptian missile batteries and put them both out of action completely. I later came to learn that this was a new U.S. rocket called the TV-camera bomb . . . still being tested in the United States. To save Israel, the U.S.A. used them against Egypt. So, the United States was now taking part in the fighting by supplying Israel with weapons still being tested, with the Maverick bomb, and many other items—to save Israel. I knew my capabilities. I did not intend to fight the entire United States of America.

On October 19, 1973, Father contacted the Syrian president, a partner in the war, and said he intended to accept a cease-fire. Father said he did not fear Israel but would not wage war with the United States. The prospect that advanced U.S. missiles could destroy Egypt's air defense system and leave the country wide open to Israeli air attacks, as in 1967, weighed on his mind.

On October 22, 1973, the cease-fire went into effect. Israel made further attempts to take Egyptian land after the cease-fire. Father explored the possibility of another military campaign to drive the Israelis back to the boundaries established on October 22. However, the United States intervened as a mediator, and in January 1974, Kissinger arrived and the first disengagement agreement was signed.

.

In the spring of 1974, President Nixon was scheduled to make a state visit to Egypt. Festivals began several days before Nixon's arrival date. Egyptians were excited because Nixon would be the first U.S. president ever to visit Egypt. There was a widespread opinion that Egypt would be well served by improved relations with the United States. Nixon's visit signaled that U.S. foreign aid to Egypt, terminated in the mid-1960s as a result of Egypt's intervention in Yemen, might be resumed. Egypt urgently needed aid to recover economically after its previous wars. Since my father had kicked the U.S.S.R.'s experts out of Egypt in 1972, it was doubtful help would be forthcoming from that quarter. The U.S. interest in Egypt was clear, since Secretary of State Henry Kissinger had been involved in shuttle diplomacy between Egypt and Israel since the October War in 1973. Father was so enamored of Kissinger that the phrase "My friend Kissinger said . . ." became rather routine in his speeches. In Egypt, people jokingly exchanged greetings with one another by saying, "Hi, my friend Kissinger!"

As for Nixon, he evidently saw the state visit to Egypt as a way to bolster his image as an international statesman and divert attention from the Watergate scandal that plagued his administration. The trip to Egypt came shortly before Nixon would resign the presidency.

Upon the visit of foreign heads of state, it was customary for the Egyptian government to ask the schools to send the children to line the streets as part of the greeting. If they had not been there, the streets still would have been packed the day Nixon arrived. Balconies were near to overflowing. There was such a sea of humans that TV cameras could not get a clear view of Father and President Nixon in the procession.

There were scores of parties, and for the first time, Father posed with Jihan and their family for photographers and for television cameramen. Unlike many other countries, where the families of rulers are considered public property, Egyptian rulers' families had been shielded from the press. From 1970, when Father became president, until the time of Nixon's visit, Jihan had been photographed at various functions, but rarely with Father. Photos of the Sadat children had never been presented in the press. However, on this occasion, President Nixon had brought his wife along. Previously, state visitors to Egypt had not been accompanied by family members. Father evidently decided that he would match Nixon's style.

Cairo was one big party. There was a cross section of Egyptians— officials, artists, intellectuals, performers, and people from virtually all strata of society.

Father believed Egypt had regained its honor in the October War and at the same time had demonstrated that it was strong enough to demand a just peace.

Henry Kissinger helped in ways that built the political alliance. When Father announced plans to reopen the Suez Canal in 1975 Kissinger would contact the White House and the Pentagon and return quickly with an offer of U.S. Navy assistance to clear the canal, an effort later joined by other major powers. Father wrote in *In Search of Identity*, "I would like here to extend our thanks to the American people, for that was a manifestation of American chivalry [i.e., the offer of help without demands for the signing of formal agreements] and an occasion on which the real face of the United States was shown."

Kissinger also became a major figure in Father's personal life when he intervened to recover 'Atif's remains from the Israelis. There was little to bring back—an identification bracelet, a pistol, a helmet, and a few bones. It was a gesture, though, that touched Father's heart. "I did not ask Henry [Kissinger] to do anything for me. He learned about my brother's death. He took it upon himself to go to the Israelis and return 'Atif's remains to me."

•

In 1974 I was twenty-five years old, and I had just earned my high school diploma. While that might not seem much of a feat to someone who completed high school at the age of seventeen or eighteen, it was a major milestone in my life. If I had not been such a rebel I might have gone through the rest of my life with only a primary school education and the equivalent of "Mrs." as my highest title.

I had been working for Hoechst, a German pharmaceutical firm. I worked there for three months as a typist. Then I became the coordinator of several personnel relations activities. Until I joined Hoechst I had gained little experience in social contacts. In the job, I learned a great deal about dealing with people and solving problems. The job made me happy and added to my feelings of independence. Yet I decided that if I was to rise professionally to the point where I could be self-sufficient, I would need a college education.

In Egypt college education was generally free, but the applicant had to overcome hurdles in order to gain admission. Vacancies in different programs were limited, so one could only specify first, second, and third preferences and hope for the best. Also, the chance of admission depended on one's high school grade record, and, in all honesty, mine was not inspiring. Despite that, I was optimistic.

The Egyptian university system had special quotas for Palestinians, for the children of parents who worked in the universities, and for children of fathers who had served Egypt in its wars. Since my father had served in the Sinai War I was able to apply for a position under the special quotas. I applied through the army's registration office, in order to qualify under the quota plan. My first choice was the communications program of Cairo University.

Somehow, though, my application was processed through the civilian registration office, and I was notified that I had been assigned to the College of Law at the University of Alexandria, which is about 180 miles from Cairo. "Oh, no!" I said, when I got the news. "I need the money from Hoechst to keep Lulee and myself going." I fully intended to continue working for Hoechst in Cairo. I got no alimony from my ex-husband, and I was determined not to ask my father for money.

I called my father's office hoping he would help me. I talked with one of his secretaries, who said he would relay my request. Soon afterward I got word from Father. "You go wherever they assign you," he instructed. No help from that quarter. I felt frustrated and hurt, because I had not asked Father for anything that was not the right of any other Egyptian. The law provided that any potential student with a job could enter a university near home.

Deciding that brooding would not solve the problem, I planned my strategy. I contacted the army's office of the registrar and requested a certificate that proved my father had, indeed, served in Egypt's military. They wrote one that attested that as president he was the commander in chief of the Egyptian army and had served in the Sinai War. With that document I then applied for a transfer to the School of Law at Ein Shams University, the second largest in Cairo. I was accepted for the transfer. And I had accomplished it all myself.

Incidentally, I was not the only member of the Sadat family who would be entering college in 1974. Jihan had earned her own British GCE diploma, which was equivalent to a high school diploma for multilingual persons, and was to enter the College of Liberal Arts at Cairo University. Gamal, my stepbrother, was to attend the same university's school of engineering.

•

A feeling had been growing among Rokaya, Rawia, and me that we needed to confront Father over the way we were being treated. Our consensus was that we should ask him directly whether he really considered us his children. If we were, then we wanted our rights, for it seemed as though we were being pushed aside systematically.

For Rokaya, being left out of Father's life at this highly eventful time was particularly galling. Part of the problem was that Father,

Rokaya, and Jihan were basically a lot alike. Father was proud and assertive. So were Rokaya and Jihan. Rokaya began skirmishes with Jihan when she first realized that she had a stepmother. That came in 1957 when Rokaya was married. She was seventeen then and Jihan was twenty-eight. Father was caught in the crossfire, and he was exceptionally vulnerable because he loved both Rokaya and Jihan. Since Rokaya was Father's first child, he felt very close to her. He had missed her while he was in prison. It was the little Rokaya who mourned the unjust treatment of her beloved father.

Rawia and I seemed to have fallen into a crack somehow, in that we had no power over him. Father, though, had a kind of power over Rokaya. He could calm her with the soothing words that re-affirmed her unique status, "My child . . . my firstborn."

There was no use, we decided, trying to go to Father's home to confront him with our grievances. We had done that over the past four years. He was secure in his own world surrounded by his new family. One does not go into the lion's own den and anger the lion.

We decided to call Father and arrange a meeting. But we faced the problem of how to accomplish it. Usually we were told he had no time for us. Sometimes it was a month before he responded. This time we would call Father individually—or, more accurately, his government secretary Fawzi Abdel Hafez, who usually answered the phone, and say that we needed to talk with him. The matter was urgent, we would say. We agreed that Father would get three calls within an hour. When he responded, we each would say that we could not meet at his house but at Rokaya's home. Father probably would be in a bind. His curiosity would be piqued, but he would be reluctant to face Rawia's temper and Rokaya's frankness.

Finally Father called me on the phone. He got the message about the meeting at Rokaya's home. "I have been sick," he said. It seemed there was a second-level message: Do not hurt me—take pity on me! He said, "I will not be able to meet you before next week." However, the next day I got a call. "I am coming tonight," he said. His curiosity had obviously got the better of him.

Looking back at this episode I think that we inherited some of Father's knack for psychological manipulation.

When Father showed up at Rokaya's place he was accompanied

by Gamal, our stepbrother. It was as though Gamal were carried as a shield that would protect Father from our wrath. "Gamal is not a boy," Father said proudly. "He is the lion of the family."

The lion of the family had to leave for a party, and Father got down to business. "What is wrong, children?"

That last word was like a battle flag. I was the first to respond. "Are we your children—or not?" My words whipped forth like arrows from a taut bow. Father looked pained. "No, you are not my children. You are the ones I depend on. Lobna, Gamal, Noha, and Jihan are my children," he said. He meant his children with Jihan. "You are adults," Father continued. "You are more like my sisters. And I can count on you." We were being lectured. And the problem was that we did not want to be Father's "sisters"—we wanted our status as daughters, with all the love, involvement, and consideration inherent in that relationship.

Father's face softened and his dark eyes radiated sincerity. "A father can always lose a child and have another, but a sister is irreplaceable." Then his voice appealed for mercy, if not pity. "Here I am, having to struggle with major decisions . . . ," he said, bowing his shoulders as though physically carrying a burden.

Rokaya and Rawia were in tears. Two grown women—Rokaya, thirty-three, and Rawia, twenty-eight—were torn that their father, who had caused the three of us anguish, should suffer himself. I, at twenty-five, remained skeptical. "We did not know," one of my sisters sobbed.

As a traditional Muslim, Father would rarely speak of his problems and feelings in this way. He was clearly speaking very openly to us and I can see that in some way he did regard us as his emotional equals, his sisters, and looked to us for support.

Father began his grand finale. "I will build a family house so everyone can be together." He went on to tell us about a project in which he intended to develop the area around the Pyramids. There would be theaters and housing. It was to be part of the Open Door Policy that Father would announce in 1974, which was designed to lure foreign investors and stimulate economic growth in Egypt. Our dream house evidently would be part of that project. However, the project was never realized because an Egyptian court ruled that tourist areas should be preserved.

Rokaya and Rawia brightened. Yet, I thought, all this is just a ploy. It is a way of diverting attention and shutting us up. After Father left the three of us had a confrontation of our own. Rokaya and Rawia got into an argument. I ran out of patience. "Both of you fought in front of him," I said. Where was the solid front we intended to present? "You cried. We were manipulated. We were duped." I was dispirited.

"It is all your fault, Rawia," Rokaya said accusingly. "You were the one who started with the tears." Poor Rawia. She had affected an increasingly tough persona, but underneath she was still the sensitive, affection-hungry child who burst into tears when personal hurts piled up.

"Well," I said, "one thing is certain. He will never meet the three of us together again." I was right. From that night onward, Father's approach was "divide and conquer." Often, he would say, "I cannot believe what I am hearing from your sister about you. . . ." He acted as though we never got together to compare notes.

I became so angry that I decided I would not kiss my father's hand again. He did not expect his children by Jihan to do it, so why should I? They just hugged and kissed him. That was what I would do. Father evidently got the message and it did hurt him, God forgive me. I could see his jaw working furiously at some times, or see one of his legs jiggling impatiently as he sat, always a sign of his restrained anger.

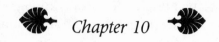

Chapter 10

A NEW START

NOT LONG after this encounter Father initiated his Open Door Policy (El Enfitah), which was designed to lure foreign investors and business to Egypt. In 1974, they began to come. Before the United States broke off relations with Egypt the life-style of Egyptians was richer. With the Open Door Policy, U.S. products began to appear in Egypt again. And when Egyptian entrepreneurs saw a market for new foreign products, they began to produce their own competing goods, often at a cheaper price.

Father's rollback of the Nasser regime's socialist policies also stimulated Egyptian productivity in other ways. We noticed that an auto shop owner who had a grubby place downstairs from my mother's apartment began to refurbish and expand his operations. One day he talked to a member of our family proudly about his new activities and confided that during the Nasser period he had hidden in a tire of his old Fiat the wealth that he had managed to accumulate. To appear wealthy was to invite government action against him. With Father's new policy encouraging economic development, however, the shop owner pulled the money from the tire and put it to work in the Egyptian economy.

Foreign investors came to Egypt to explore the new opportunities. One of these investors was a Syrian, Nader Bayzid, who wanted to open a construction company. He had left his native country at age sixteen and had been living in Germany and Spain. He was a wealthy man in his own right. We met at a barbecue in the home of Yusif Wahby, the dean of Egyptian theater. Nader was a trim, athletic type who looked as though he went jogging twice a day (I later found out that he did). He was also something of an international type. I later learned that, in addition to his native Arabic, he spoke five languages fluently—English, French, Spanish, German, and Italian.

•

After the initial encounter with Nader Bayzid at the Wahby party, he tried to get in touch with me. I had not given him a phone number because under our custom it would not have been proper for him to call a divorced woman at her mother's home, where I was living, and ask for a date. He would have been expected to meet the family first and then seek permission to see me. He circumvented this by working through a mutual friend, who relayed messages.

Nader sent flowers to the house, but Mother did not suspect anything as my colleagues at the German pharmaceutical firm sent flowers on virtually every occasion. So when the flowers arrived, my mother seemed to assume that they were from my co-workers. If she thought otherwise, she did not say anything. Neither did I make an issue of them.

The persistent Nader learned from friends where I would go out with groups for dinner. Wherever I went, he started to show up, too. Somehow he always managed to get a seat next to me at the table. A handsome man, Nader was about five feet seven. He had sharply defined features. His hair was silvery and his eyes were light brown. My eyes focused on his smile and his nice, even teeth. He carried himself in a casual way. I liked the fact that he treated everyone kindly, even his driver.

I found myself thinking more and more about Nader. We had not talked about romance, love, or a future together, though we were often alone when he gave me rides to or from the dinners with friends. To avoid complications with my mother I had Nader pick me up at a corner near my mother's home and leave me there upon my return. During this low-key courtship, Nader never said "I love you." He was more subtle. As he drove he would sing songs whose message could not be denied. One of the songs, popularized by the famous Egyptian singer Om Kalsoum, included the phrase "If you love, why deny it?"

•

Due to Father's presidency, life became increasingly restricted. Not only could we not see our father when we wanted to, we got orders about whom we could meet and where we could go. Bodyguards assigned by my father shadowed us. Father always had a report on his desk the next day telling him where we had been, whom we had seen, and what we had been doing. I felt that a box was being built around me and that, like a strange torture device, it was becoming smaller and smaller.

The idea of seeking my own identity and doing it in a foreign land was what attracted me to Nader Bayzid at first. He had a company in Spain. I could see myself escaping to a happier future in a foreign land. Such are the dreams that make up romantic novels and appeal to those who are not satisfied with their real lives.

After Nader and I had been going out for about six months we began to discuss marriage. It happened one night after we dined out with friends and all of our companions had left.

Our courtship had been a well-kept secret. Neither my mother, father, nor sisters knew I was seeing Nader Bayzid. After my divorce from Ezz I did not think of marrying again. However, a divorced woman in Egypt is not likely to remain unmarried. Rawia had been divorced twice, although Rokaya remained married. In Egypt a divorced woman is not able to get into circulation as easily as in Western countries. Casual contacts are restricted. My friends tried to play matchmaker. Even Jihan applied pressure. "Have you not found an appropriate suitor yet?" she teased. "We will find one for you." I decided, though, that if I did find a man whom I would consider marrying, *I* would make the selection rather than trust an arranged marriage again.

Nader impressed me as warm, intellectual, and compassionate. He knew I still bore psychological scars from my first marriage. "You cannot be afraid of all men because you had one bad experience," he said. "Why do you have to keep reminding yourself of your ex-husband? All men are different. I am different from him. And another man would be different from me." Nader's patience with me seemed endless. He was affectionate but never demanding. We had long, frank talks about all sorts of topics. He treated me like a partner and a grown woman, a decided difference from the way I had been treated by my ex-husband.

The more time I spent with Nader, the more I knew I wanted him and would be willing to do anything for him. He was a dream of a man. I loved to dance with him, for he made a woman feel she was the world's most graceful dancer. Also, he had a simple style, though he was educated and widely traveled. An engineer and head of his own construction company, he was also prosperous. But he was equally comfortable eating the food of the Egyptian poor and dining in elegant restaurants.

In temperament, Nader proved a good match for me. I think fast and talk fast. Being with a talkative, assertive man would have driven me crazy. Nader, however, tended to listen quietly and speak infrequently. He offered me something that the principal man in my life, my father, did not. Although both were responsible men, Father's attitude was, "Go your way, but just do not bother me with your mistakes." In contrast Nader seemed to say, "I feel responsible for you. You are not alone anymore."

"I want to marry you," Nader said. It was a straightforward proposal. I knew he had been married to a German woman, who gave him three sons. He continued, "Camelia, you are a warm and true person. I want to share my life with you."

The big problem was breaking the news to my family, especially my mother and father. Nader was Syrian. Egyptian families do not like their daughters to marry foreigners, since the husband might take the daughter out of the country. Also, the children would be of mixed parentage. If the prospective spouse were of another religion, that would be an even greater problem. In my case, though, my potential second husband was a Muslim.

I feared that if I approached Father first, he might reject Nader as a son-in-law. And when Father said no, it was an irreversible no. So I decided to approach Rokaya. I went to her and told her, "I do not know where this proposal will lead, but he wants to meet you as my eldest sister. Also, I would value your appraisal of Nader."

Rokaya met Nader twice and became very supportive. Nader's charm no doubt helped win her over. "Even though I am older than you," he told Rokaya, "I respect you as my elder sister, and I kiss your hand." Rokaya could not resist that. Soon Rokaya and her husband and Nader and I became a foursome. Rokaya and Amin entertained us in their home. And we went out together. Yet Mother and Father were still not aware of my courtship. Rokaya and I decided to approach my parents separately but on the same day.

"I have examined Nader at length," Rokaya informed Mother. "I have found him to be a suitable prospective husband." Mother expressed great happiness for me. Nader, who was not there, called later and spoke to my mother. "Mother, I am coming to ask your blessing," he said, "and I hope Camelia's father will accept me, too." If she had been a less sturdy woman my mother might have swooned at the thought of gaining such a respectful, courteous son-in-law.

We decided to put off the meeting with Father until the next day. This was in April 1975. We met Father at one of the presidential residences, in Barrage, which is about fifteen miles from Cairo and near the Nile Delta. When we met, Rokaya broached the topic. "Father, there is a man who has proposed to Camelia. I have come to know him well. Amin and I have been with him."

Father puffed silently on his pipe, looking off into the distance. He often did that. He looked at the sky or beyond you—but not at you. He seemed to be reflecting on what he heard. I remained very quiet, watching his face for some sign of his thoughts. Rokaya did not mention Nader's Syrian origin. I decided to bring it up, to see what Father would say.

"I do not care where he was born, so long as he is Muslim," Father said when he finally spoke. "He is Muslim, is he not?" We assured Father that Nader was Muslim. Father is more open-minded than I would have thought, I told myself.

"When will you have time to announce the engagement?" Rokaya asked Father.

Father was under the impression that I had known Nader for only two months, the time in which Rokaya and her husband had been "evaluating" my suitor. "Camelia, you should go out with him till you are sure you know him," he advised. "Two months is not enough. You do not want to rush into a marriage only to have another divorce. When you are sure of your decision, I will be available to announce the engagement."

Nader and I became engaged two months later at a party given at Father's beach house. I was twenty-six years old and Nader was thirty-nine. During the summer Nader and I traveled to Europe along with Rokaya and her husband—and with Father's consent. We spent five weeks touring Germany, France, and Italy. Back in Egypt Nader got along well with members of the family. He charmed my mother. He called her and asked, "Mother, do you have yogurt in the house for me?" When he arrived, Mother was in the midst of preparing a huge meal for him. "I do not want you slaving away for me, Mother," he said. She protested that she was preparing only "a little something" to prevent him from starving.

I married Nader in December 1975. The wedding reflected the schism between Father's first and second families.

The signing of the wedding contract took place at my father's residence in Giza. Father, Jihan, my stepsisters, and my stepbrother were in attendance. My uncles, on Father's side of the famiy, also came. However, my mother did not attend, because she was not welcome in Jihan's home. Neither were any members of Mother's family invited.

Nader had planned a big wedding party after the signing of the contract. He rented all three floors of the Versailles Palace restaurant. He wanted to make up for the joyless first wedding party I had experienced with Ezz, which had coincided with the break-up of the political pact between Egypt and Syria that had upset Father so much. I was on top of the world because we were entertained by renowned belly dancers, singers, and musicians. I remember it as one of the best nights of my life.

The fact that my father and Jihan and their family chose not to attend upset Nader. He had invited them all. Perhaps they did not come because my mother would attend. However, Father's brothers joined in, as did Rokaya and her husband, Rawia, and various other family members. Nader also invited all the government officials whom he had met in Europe. My father would take umbrage over those invitations later.

•

Nader continued to travel back and forth between Egypt and various countries in Europe as he had prior to our wedding.

One day I visited Nader's parents, who had moved some years earlier to Egypt from Syria. Nader's mother, while working in the kitchen, told me, "I was very upset when he told me he would marry you."

"Why?" I asked.

"I thought you would take him from his German wife and their children or mistreat the children," she said. "However, I learned from the children what a fine person you were."

Her words about his "wife" stunned me. I truly believed I was

Nader's only wife. "He was divorced from his German wife," I responded after a pause.

"No, Nader never was divorced," his mother said. Although men in Egypt can have more than one wife, I never would agree knowingly to such an arrangement. If what she said was true, Nader enjoyed the comforts of another wife, family, and home when he traveled to Europe.

Within a week, I encountered another shock. Nader had given me an ornate wedding ring. I decided to have the diamond that was the centerpiece reset in a simple platinum mount. The jeweler, a friend, examined the stone and asked, "Why do you wish to put this stone in a mount that is worth more than the stone itself?" I thought he must have been confused. But he informed me that the main stone was a variety of zirconium—hardly a diamond. "Please give me the ring," I said. I did not care to explain that it was the wedding ring from my new husband. I returned home with the ring.

Two days later, another revelation surprised me. I got a call from one of Father's secretaries, Adnan Refa-at, who said he intended to send a letter to me by a private courier. I probed to find out what this mysterious matter was about. I remember Adnan as a very kind man. He told me, somewhat haltingly, that there had been a complaint that Nader had not paid for the wedding party—about 4,000 Egyptian pounds. Nader allegedly had told the manager of the restaurant, "Look, I brought all those important people to your restaurant. That should be worth something. Take half, or I will not pay anything."

When Nader returned to Cairo, I put before him the ring, the bill for the party, and a note. The note said, in essence, "Because I am your wife, I accept your cheating—the fact that you are not divorced and the fact that you gave me a fake ring—but if you do not pay the bill for the wedding party, neither my father nor anyone else will show you any mercy."

Nader paid the bill, and acted like a man who had been beaten. After a week, he finally spoke about my note. "You did not give me a chance to talk about these things. Who said I would not pay for the party? The manager overcharged me, and I was negotiating. But because of your pressure, I have paid him the full amount."

About the ring, Nader said, "How would I know the person who sold me the ring would cheat me?" I could accept that. Then he got around to the issue of his other wife. "I am keeping her so that she will take care of the boys and not bring in a stepfather for them. Our marriage is over, and she accepts that."

I truly loved Nader and I accepted his explanations, for the moment. He also doted on my daughter. When Nader and I were married my mother suggested that Lulee live with her. Lulee was nine years old at the time. Nader, however, insisted that my daughter live with us. He adored her, and she returned the feeling. She called him Daddy, as did his own sons.

I had been married for about two months when my father began to display a marked dislike for my husband. Father's behavior led to a sequence of events that showed his hard side. And the events turned my life upside down again. I got a call from my father not long after my marriage. He was angry about something, and it turned out to be Nader. "This husband of yours has been exploiting the Sadat name," he said.

"In what way?" I asked.

"Well, the prime minister got a report from customs that your husband put your name on a shipment of goods in order to avoid paying the import duties," he said.

"You should investigate the truth of the report," I said. "If there is something wrong, you should put him in jail."

There had been a shipment. It was furniture that Nader had sent from Spain to help set up my apartment. I held receipts from a transport broker showing that the fees had been paid and that everything was in order. It was obvious to me that some form of petty envy had caused someone to initiate the rumor. Nader was not only handsome but also wealthy. He moved on a grand scale. We had been traveling abroad. Our life-style was conspicuous enough to stir invidious comparison.

What the rumormongers did not know, though, was that I held the receipts. That was really no protection, though, since Father jealously guarded his public reputation. And what the public believed was often more important to him than reality. He raised hell when there was a rumor, but he did nothing—least of all, apologize—when the rumors that gave birth to his furies were disproved. This was not an insignificant idiosyncrasy on my father's part, as two of his brothers knew too well. Even before Father became the vice-president of Egypt, in 1966, there had been a rumor that my uncle Esmat was implicated in the corruption of a company in which he worked. Acting on the rumor, without any confirmation, Father had him put in jail. Under the Nasser regime people were often subjected to arbitrary arrest and imprisonment. The fact that Esmat developed diabetes while he was in jail did not soften Father's position. Later, after a trial, a court found that there was no case against Esmat. He was released after being in jail for three months.

In 1972 after Father became president, there was another rumor that his elder brother Talaat had smuggled valuables into Egypt while returning from a trip to Saudi Arabia. He, too, was summarily ordered to jail by my father, on what appeared to be a capricious accusation. Father's order led to Uncle Talaat's being jailed for six months. There was no trial. Since the government scheduled no investigation of the accusation, Talaat could have languished there forever. Although Father had banned arbitrary arrests without trial, he later referred to his action against Talaat in many speeches, saying, "The only exception to my rule against arbitrary arrest came in relation to a member of my own family." Father evidently sought to prove that his integrity as a foe of corruption was above reproach.

The jail in which Talaat stayed was so dilapidated that the government decided it should be razed. Because there was no other facility for all the prisoners, the government ruled that those who had been imprisoned the longest should be freed. Consequently, Uncle Talaat regained his freedom, but not because he had been tried or because my father had showed any compassion.

I remember that during Talaat's imprisonment I pleaded with Father for his brother's release. I said I had heard Talaat, like Esmat, showed symptoms of becoming diabetic. Father turned his head, refusing to look at me. That was one of the signals that meant, "I do not want to hear any more of this. If you persist, it is at your own risk." From experience, I knew that if I pressed the issue he would lash back in a fury. It was not predictable how far he might go. The fact that I was a blood relative was no protection.

As for Uncle Talaat, who loves and reveres his brother, he was badly shaken by the experience. Afterward, whenever he talked about that time in his life, his voice and manner took on a cowed quality.

I could not easily understand that hard side of my father, who was often so solicitous of his family and the Egyptian people. Father, honest and exceptionally strict, seemed to feel that when something touched his family he had to be the toughest. Although he was not the eldest male in his family, he used to punish close kin who made mistakes. He seemed to be telling the alleged offenders, "You are ruining my reputation as a good and honest man." He showed no mercy and would not listen to opposing views.

.

During those days, I did not understand what caused Father's exceptional irritability toward Nader. It seemed irrational to me. But, as I have said, we members of Sadat's first family knew of his political activities only through what we learned through the media or via Cairo's gossip network. We were not privy to information that Father was devoting most of his energy to evolving an initiative to solve the uneasy confrontation between Israel and Egypt.

From what I understand today, Father sought to distance himself from distracting problems so that he could focus on major problems. I believe the rumors about Nader upset Father because they constituted a wasteful preoccupation. Dealing with petty family matters would divert his valuable limited energies.

The rumors would also have caused Father anxiety on another score. If he dared to make a major deviation from the anti-Israeli confrontational strategy of the past, he could not appear before his people or the opposition as weak or indecisive in any aspect. That had been part of his strategy in the 1973 war—he believed leadership that appeared less than strong, confident, and resolute could lose a campaign before it began.

One sweet memory I recall from this strained period resulted from a visit by Father and my stepbrother, Gamal, to Mother's home to see Rawia, who had been injured in a car accident. When Mother went to the door she was excited, because Father had not visited her in eight years. He entered and put one arm around Mother's shoulders as they walked to Rawia's room. "How old we are getting," he groaned and jokingly walked with the stoop of an old man. They agreed that their premature aging resulted from the problems their children had caused them. Gamal talked with my mother later and called her Mama, which delighted her, for she considers him her son and calls him so when they meet.

•

One day, I was called to Father's house concerning a new rumor about Nader. "I hear that he has been taking money for construction projects and that he has not delivered what he contracted," Father said. Nader had set up his own construction company in Egypt under the Open Door Policy and was quite active. "Also, I hear that he has manipulated the company's records to cover his trail."

That day Osman Ahmed Osman was with my father. Once a government minister of housing and construction, Osman was a major figure in the Egyptian construction industry. His son was married to my youngest stepsister, Jihan. Furthermore, he was a close friend of my father.

"Why do you not let Osman investigate Nader if you think something is wrong," I challenged Father. He accepted the challenge.

Osman responded softly. "Siadet el-Rayes, do not listen to rumors. I will look into this."

Even this, though, was an infringement of Nader's rights. Ordinarily the government would face disapproval if it went about nosing into Egyptians' business, but Nader had lost some of his rights simply by being married to me.

Osman later reported back to my father. He had found no evidence of misdeeds, he said. It was true, he said, that Nader did not deliver some projects on time, but that was not unusual in Egypt. When contracts provided for the payment of penalties for late delivery of a completed project, Nader paid the penalties, which was in keeping with business custom in the industry.

Instead of acknowledging that he had wronged my husband and me, Father renewed the attack. It was the fourth time I had been called to Father's office about Nader. I waited for him to begin. "I cannot stand him," Father said, his eyes as intense as burning coals. "If you want to be his wife you cannot be my daughter at the same time. He is causing me too much trouble."

What was I to say? Nader had been accused falsely. Nothing had been proved against him. If Father refused to listen further till evidence was presented, there would have been no problem. But that did not fit with Father's self-image as a "good and honest man" who was a keeper of the public trust. There was an added tension involved because Nader was a Syrian, and political relations were not that good with Syria at the time. However, I believe that if I, the daughter of the Egyptian president, had married an American or a Frenchman or some other foreign national, my father would also have been especially sensitive to the resentment of those who surrounded him.

"I do not want him here," Father stated. "If you want to go with him, go!"

I looked at him incredulously. Was this the same father who threatened to disown me when I wanted to divorce Ezz? Then I thought about myself and suddenly I thought of things that I had tried not to think about before. I remembered the story of the marriage to his other wife, the incident of the ring, and the bill for the wedding reception. And I remembered noting that he had grown cooler, less attentive, after we were married. While we were on our honeymoon, he had planned a business trip, and when I protested, he had responded edgily, saying, "You think that marriage is always staying at home? I have my business to tend—a marriage is a business, too." Had Nader been opportunistic in marrying me? The thoughts buzzed in my head. And I knew that if I stayed with Nader, no matter where we went, Father would not leave me in peace. It seemed that I was destined to have only one man in my life—my father. "I will leave him." I said finally.

It was not an easy decision. I had loved Nader and his children and he had loved my daughter. And in Egypt to have failed once in a marriage was serious; twice can destroy your reputation. You are grist for the rumor mills. I was not sure how I would cope with it.

·

I could never break the news to Nader myself. I asked Father if he would have his secretary contact my husband, who was then living in Alexandria, while I stayed in Cairo. At least I would not have to look Nader in the eye. Father's secretary talked with Nader and arranged a date to sign the papers for the divorce.

It was, I think, the most difficult time in my life. "Tell her, 'I divorce thee,' " Nader was told. He repeated the statement. "Tell him, 'I accept,' " I was told. I repeated the statement. It was 1977. At age twenty-eight I was once again a divorced woman. I felt a heaviness in my heart. It represented the breakup of my home. I had been raised to believe it was better to go the limit in order to try for a compromise. Then there was the matter of my financial security. I also did not know how to break the news of the divorce to Mother, who adored Nader, or to Lulee. My daughter, then eleven, kept asking, "When is Daddy coming back?" All I could tell her was that he was away on a trip. Sharing the news that he would never come back would be painful to both of us. I just could not cope with more at the time. The future seemed bleak.

.

A week later Nader sold his company and left Egypt. In a way, this must have been a relief to him. As the son-in-law of the president he was under almost daily scrutiny. After the divorce Nader treated me well. Since I had, in effect, initiated the divorce, he was not obligated to pay me alimony, but he gave it to me voluntarily for a year. Also, he had joined my father in buying a condominium for me. The title had been put in my name. Nader did not dispute my title to the condominium. In addition, he gave me a piece of land, in my name, one that his business had acquired. It was worth about 100,000 Egyptian pounds (about $70,000 at the time). He did not challenge my title to the land. I thought I would be able to live on the money from the land until I was able to get another job. Then my father's younger brother Zein showed up to crush that plan. "There is no way you will keep that land," he said. "What would the public say if it became known that you had such a valuable piece of land? You must give it back, or you will be put in jail by your father," Zein ordered.

It was hard to tell, from what others said, whether or not my father had really ordered this. I could see him sending me to jail on some charge or another. I remembered the bad luck of my uncles Esmat and Talaat, Father's own blood brothers. I am not closer to my father than Talaat, I thought. I could see myself being featured in Father's speeches as the third Sadat whom he had, as president, thrown into prison to prove that he was a good and honest man. I caved in and signed the land back over to Nader's representative in Egypt.

I had sufficient alimony money to live on. But I knew that would not last forever, so I sought out the manager of the Hoechst pharmaceutical company, for which I had worked earlier. There I found that someone else had preceded me, allegedly speaking on behalf of President Sadat. The manager said that Rokaya's husband had been to see him, saying that if I showed up to ask for a job my father wanted him to refuse me. I did not think it was Father's will at all, though at the time I could not be absolutely sure. "If your father does not want you working here," the manager said, "then I cannot hire you. On the other hand, if he gives his permission, then I definitely will hire you."

After that I tried to call Father. I could not talk to him, so I left messages. I got no reply. Then I sent a letter. I got no reply. When the rumormongers speak, Father, you listen. When I call for help, you do not. Where is my place in your heart? I was hurt and angry.

•

It was then Ramadan. I received a call from one of my father's secretaries telling me I was invited to break the fast with the president. Ramadan is a celebration of the month in which the angel Gabriel brought the holy Koran to Mohammed the Prophet. The time of Ramadan changes from year to year, because it is governed by the moon. Muslims observe Ramadan by fasting from dawn till sunset. They take no food or drink during this time. It is intended to help them remember the misery and suffering of the poor. Neither do the observers of Ramadan smoke. They offer five prayers a day and read verses from the Koran. They also make payments to charities, typically amounting to two and a half percent of their annual income. Also, when it is possible, Muslims make their pilgrimage to the holy city of Mecca.

The invitation was no sign of an improved relationship with my father. It was customary for members of the family to be invited for breakfast after fasting during Ramadan. I decided to call and decline, saying that I was ill.

Two days later Father's personal secretary, Fawzi Abdel Hafez, showed up. Fawzi had been with Father since 1954. He was a man who turned a brusque face to the world. But I called him Uncle. "Your father is angry with you," he said. "He does not believe that you were ill."

"Perhaps the next time I should send a note from my doctor excusing me," I said bitterly.

Fawzi said, "Your father is disturbed because he has been told that you continue to have a business alliance with your ex-husband even though he has left Egypt. He also understands that your ex-husband is angry because you have not returned the land he gave you." Will this never end? I thought. "I have had nothing to do with Nader since he left," I said icily. "As for the land, I gave it back under your orders." If Father did not know about that, it meant he had not received my recent letter.

Fawzi pressed on. "Your father hears you are in business, using his name . . ." That was entirely too much.

"You get me divorced," I screamed. "You prevent me from working. You force me to put up my jewelry as collateral for a loan so I can live. I have the papers for my alimony and for my loan. I can prove it all."

Fawzi sagged. It was the first time I had seen him, Fawzi the tough, look ashamed. But I did not quit there. "You keep meddling in my life," I raged. "I have had enough. You must quit it! Quit listening to rumors. What I tell you, I can prove. Everything!"

My eyes met Fawzi's. "I hope you are honest enough to tell my father what you have seen and what you know. It seems he is isolated from reality and believes all sorts of poisonous rumors against me, his daughter." The embarrassed Fawzi excused himself and left.

Two days later, Fawzi called. "Your father had not known about your situation," he said. I was exasperated. There was no way he could not have known. I could hardly scratch an itch at night without Father having a report on his desk the next morning telling when and where I did it.

"Your father has provided collateral to cover your loan," Fawzi informed me. "Your jewelry will be returned to you. Also, he wants you to know that we have called the Hoechst manager to tell him that your brother-in-law did not have the right to speak for him." The latter news meant I would get my job back.

"The president said that he will call you when he returns from a trip," Fawzi said.

My anger was unrelieved. I will be waiting for that call, I thought.

True to his word, Father arranged a meeting with me at his house in Mit Abul-Kum when he returned. I alone was invited. It seemed he was ready for a heart-to-heart talk—but, as usual, his version of a heart-to-heart talk was to tell me what he wanted me to know. We were seated side by side on a swing in the garden. He had an arm around me as we slowly moved back and forth. I could smell his after-shave, something delicately fragrant, like Monsieur Givenchy. Father's manner was very conciliatory. "It was your mistake," he said, "that you married Nader. That started all the rumors. If it were not for Nader, our relationship would have been very happy, I think."

The underlying message was: You have made a mistake, but I am kind enough to forgive you. He looked into the distance. I studied his face, so much like my own—the warm earth tones of his skin, the finely defined bones in his cheeks. Maybe it is because we are so much alike that we have so many troubles, I thought. I tried to frame my thoughts to reply.

Getting a word in while Father was talking was not easy. He talked constantly. He was diplomatic about how he did it, but you could not get a chance to answer. Every time you tried to break in he would block you with a personal compliment. Father paused, then spoke again. "We all make mistakes," he said philosophically, "but life continues. . . ." He concluded by offering to send me on a trip to Europe to give me time to settle my mind. My daughter, Lulee, should go with me, he said.

Maybe it is a bribe to ease his conscience, I thought, but I could use time away. It was the first time I realized I would gain nothing by confronting Father. He would always win.

I felt that I had tried to define my relationship with him but his swings of mood had often thrown me. At one time he would be warm and affectionate, appreciative that my upbringing had taught me to behave in the traditional courteous ways. At other times he would be cold and distant. For my own peace of mind, I had to step away from the conflict and search out my own individual identity as a woman, as a Muslim, and as my father's daughter.

Perhaps with enough distance between me and both Father and Egypt, I could gain some perspective and get my life under control. I realized I would need to complete a college education in order to gain that independence. Perhaps, the thought arose a second time, I might have to leave my beloved country and start an independent life of my own. During the next few months I thought long and hard, and finally, painfully, made the decision to finish my education abroad. I would start my life again as an independent woman, a thing I could never do in my own country.

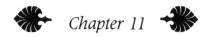

Chapter 11

THE WORLD STATESMAN

FATHER'S PEACE INITIATIVE of February 1971, which he directed at both Israel and its patron, the United States, never gained a serious audience, but I believe it was the first major milestone on his historic trip to Jerusalem and Camp David.

I think Father believed that Israel embraced with unfortunate dogmatism the Security Theory of its renowned leader David Ben-Gurion. This theory held that peace should be imposed on the Arabs by force of arms. But as Father would later argue to President Carter:

Peace cannot be imposed. If imposed, it will cease to be peace, inasmuch as one party dictates its terms to the other. Israel has not so far succeeded in dictating her terms in spite of our terrible 1967 defeat. And we, in spite of our victory in 1973, have not been able to dictate our terms to Israel. The idea of imposing peace and secure borders should therefore be discarded.

At the same time, Father felt that until Henry Kissinger's advent in the Middle East the United States was not forthcoming on a negotiated solution of Middle Eastern problems. Father thought the John Foster Dulles policy under Eisenhower was very shortsighted. At that time the U.S. government had little tolerance for either nonalignment or nonconformists like Nasser. Dulles's position was, You are either totally with us, or you are against us. The Kennedy and Johnson presidencies did not entertain serious thoughts of a negotiated settlement between the Arab states and Israel. Besides, the Vietnam War bound U.S. foreign policy to the Far East. Secretary of State Rogers, under Nixon, appeared to be in the thrall of Israel. Then, after Kissinger launched his shuttle diplomacy the Watergate crisis paralyzed the Nixon regime. The Ford administration became a caretaker government after Nixon resigned. Consequently, Ford lacked a mandate for major foreign policy initiatives.

During Father's emergence as a world figure in the mid-1970s, I think that Henry Kissinger became a catalyst, perhaps unintentionally. In matters of foreign policy and in the international media, Kissinger helped build the image of President Sadat as a stable and reasonable person. Unfortunately, even now the Western press tends to stereotype Arab leaders as fanatical visionaries who are often self-serving and potentially volatile, unreliable, and dangerous. But in the company of Kissinger the world saw an urbane Sadat who was well dressed, articulate—even in English—and possessed of a sense of humor and the ability to handle the media. At that time the world did not know Father as a studious man who had been a communications specialist for most of his adult life.

•

When Father met with the new U.S. president, Carter, he told the American leader about his peace strategy:

I told President Carter that Israel should be given all the guarantees she wants. If she wanted to have every Israeli citizen armed with a tank and an aircraft, and got such armanents from the United States, we could not object—provided, of course, that those weapons were used within her own, not other people's territory. We would never object to anything Israel wants, whether from the United States, the Soviet Union, or the UN Security Council, and in any form she wants—whether it is a United Nations force to police the borders; demilitarized zones on a reciprocal basis, or a common defense pact with the United States. . . . We cannot have any bargaining over the rights of the Palestinian people or over one inch of the Arab territories seized in 1967. Only thus can a permanent and just peace be achieved.

Father developed a rapport with President Carter. About this, Father said in *In Search of Identity*, "President Carter knew of the tremendous psychological barrier that separated the two sides. . . . [He] is true to himself and true to others. It is because he is so honest with himself that he can be honest with others. . . . I find that I am dealing with a man who understands what I want, a man impelled by the power of religious faith and lofty values—a farmer, like me."

Father wrote, though, that there were others like Syria's President Hafez al-Assad who argued that nothing in the Middle Eastern formula had changed—that Israel did not want to solve the problem and only sought to gain time and an advantage; that the United States did not want to solve the problem either and even if it did, would not know how.

Father's thinking often reflected a tendency to view issues in a moral context. In this case, he wrote that he had decided that if he ignored his duty to protect future generations from more warfare and suffering, he "would have done wrong. I would be sinning both against myself and against my God, who would call me to account for everything I did."

During this time Father traveled to confer with foreign leaders about the problems of the Middle East. Rumania's President Nicolae Ceausescu, who had talked extensively with Israel's leader Menachem Begin, told Father, "Let me state categorically to you that [Begin] wants peace." Father regarded Ceausescu's counsel seriously, and saw an opening for a new effort that might be successful.

After considerable reflection Father focused on a daring move. On November 9, 1977, he informed the Egyptian parliament, the People's Assembly, that he would be willing to go even to Israel if it would help obtain peace between Israelis and Egyptians. Afterward, he expressed amusement that some people thought he had made a slip of the tongue in saying he would go to Israel or had perhaps got confused while making his speech.

Soon, however, the U.S. ambassador arrived with an invitation from Begin to visit Israel and address the Knesset. Father had two days to prepare his speech. His foreign minister balked at the initiative (his resignation was later accepted).

Knowing the risk of his momentous journey, Father also took time to write his own epitaph, which he would leave behind, just in case.

·

The trip to Lod Airport in Israel on November 19, 1977, represented a flight of less than forty minutes, but it easily held as much drama as the first U.S. space trip to the moon. It became a major media event, beamed live via satellite to a world that waited to see what Anwar el-Sadat's audacity would produce.

In Cairo there was saturation coverage by all the media. TV

coverage came live from Israel. My sisters and I gathered at Mother's home to watch the spectacle. We all had goose bumps as the Egypt Air jet rolled to a stop and Father emerged after a brief delay, looking somewhat disconcertedly across the mass of Israelis who were there to meet him. As he descended from the plane, we could see him begin to smile. "Look how he is enjoying all this!" I exclaimed. Father chatted amiably before our eyes with Mrs. Golda Meir. Then he joked with Moshe Dayan, Abba Eban, and General Ariel Sharon. We expected to hear a bullet at any minute. There was an unexpressed fear that Father might be killed. As was her custom during this period, Mother prayed five times a day. In each of her prayers she pleaded, "God, please bring Anwar safely back to us." When the television announced that Father had left the airport en route to the King David Hotel in the Israeli section of Jerusalem, we breathed a collective sigh of relief.

On November 20, 1977, Father went to pray at the al-Aqsa Mosque. Afterward he went to make his historic address before the Israeli Knesset. The first minutes of Father's speech set the tone for his initiative:

We must all rise above all forms of obsolete theories of superiority, and the most important thing is never to forget that infallibility is the prerogative of God alone. If I said that I wanted to avert from all the Arab people the horrors of shocking and destructive wars, I must sincerely declare before you that I have the same feelings and bear the same responsibility toward all and every man on earth, and certainly toward the Israeli people. Any life that is lost in war is a human life, be it that of an Arab or an Israeli. A wife who becomes a widow is a human being entitled to a happy life, whether she be an Arab or an Israeli. Innocent children who are devoid of the care and compassion of their parents are ours. They are ours, be they living on Arab or Israeli land. They command our full responsibility to afford them a comfortable life today and tomorrow.

Father also dealt with Israel's concern for security within its borders:

In all sincerity, I tell you we welcome you among us with full security and safety. This in itself is a tremendous turning point, one of the landmarks of a decisive historical change. We used to reject you. We had our reasons and our fears, yes. We refused to meet with you, anywhere, yes.

. . . Yet today I tell you and I declare it to the whole world that we accept to live with you in permanent peace based on justice. We do not want to encircle you or be encircled ourselves by destructive missiles ready for launching, nor by the shells of grudges and hatreds.

Father called for an end to the state of belligerence, the return of lands occupied by Israel in the 1967 war, direct negotiations between Egypt and Israel, and a solution to the problem of the Palestinians.

The trip to Israel also had a family significance for Father. His daughter Noha gave birth to a girl during his trip abroad. The birth caused unrest in our part of his family, since the press raved about the birth of Sadat's "first grandchild."

•

In *In Search of Identity* Father said that he was prepared to offer his resignation as president if he returned to Cairo and found that the Egyptian people did not support his initiative. However, on November 21, 1977, nearly five million Egyptians turned out to receive their bold leader with great warmth and enthusiasm.

Before Father returned I called his office and asked for an appointment with him. I was proud of his courage and his effort on behalf of peace and wished to greet and congratulate him personally. However, one of his staff told me that he would not be available for quite a while.

Rokaya, on the other hand, went to Father's home in Cairo the day he got back. She had trouble getting past the guards, but eventually they admitted her to the house. "Father was in a very good mood," Rokaya reported. "He was joking with everyone. Jihan and their children, Jihan's relatives, and some friends were all there." And, I thought, once again Rokaya, Rawia, and I were excluded. Only, Rokaya had literally forced herself into the gathering.

Earlier in the day Mother and I had called back and forth by phone to discuss the TV coverage of Father's return to Egypt. Later I went to Mother's house. The streets were clogged with people shouting excitedly about "peace" and "no more war." No peace treaty had been signed, but the people inferred that this was the beginning of the end of hostilities with Israel. Motorists began honking their horns in a joyful cacophony, and as I returned from

Mother's house, I joined in. This is for you, Father, I thought. I hope you hear it. It is the only way I can express my pride in you, my president.

Afterward Father went to the People's Assembly to report that he had returned with a two-item agenda: that the October War would be the last one with Israel and that there should be direct negotiation over the security concerns of both Israel and Egypt. Only a handful of the 360 members of the People's Assembly objected. In the Arab world, though, many voices were raised against Father's "treachery." Reportedly, even Syrian government officials called for his assassination. Leaders of a few nations in the Middle East encouraged Father to pursue his initiative, but most of them declined to go public with their support for fear of complicating their own situations.

The rest of the events that flowed from Father's peace initiative are written in history. President Carter invited Father and Menachem Begin to the States for the face-to-face negotiations that Father had insisted were integral to a solution. The press reported the arduous meetings and Carter's persistence in trying to lead Father and Begin to an understanding of how they could agree without sacrificing their principles. We saw Father on TV. Though he assumed a relaxed pose, I could imagine what a psychological drain the experience must have been. I never doubted that he would succeed.

The Camp David accords, as I understand them, held promise of improvements between Egypt and Israel. The state of war would be ended. Diplomats would be exchanged. The borders would be opened to travel. Egypt's territories that had been seized by Israel in the Six-Day War were to be repatriated. Israeli settlements in those Egyptian territories were to be abandoned—and that was a major point of contention.

The accords did not provide a solution for the Palestinians. The territorial problems of Syria and Jordan, which had lost, respectively, the Golan Heights and the West Bank, were not solved. Camp David was regarded as an ongoing process, and the negotiators left it to Syria and Jordan to join in talks at a later time to resolve those territorial problems. An agreement concerning a freeze on further Israeli settlements in the West Bank was abortive because the Israelis later disputed the meaning of the text. Because of those shortcomings, various Middle Eastern factions would vigorously reject the Camp David process and bitterly attack my father.

At the signing of the Camp David accords the obvious affection President Carter showed for my father touched me greatly. This mutual respect holds a lot of promise, I thought. Carter treated Menachem Begin cordially at the end of the ceremonies, but Begin, who tried to appear animated, just looked stiff to me. And Carter's enthusiasm for Begin seemed forced, as contrasted with his spontaneous affection for Father. My inferences about Carter's feelings for my father were borne out by his memoirs, *Keeping Faith*, published later, which gave his account of the Camp David experience.

•

After the Camp David accords, Father turned his energies and attention to Egypt's domestic affairs. Ninety-six percent of Egypt is desert, and the housing pressure in the big cities is tremendous. Building new cities was an attempt to solve this problem. In 1978 Father opened the city of al-Asher Min Ramadan (the name signifying the date of the 1973 October War), and in 1979 he made the Port Said area into a free zone for investors and industry. In 1980 he opened the city of Sadat, on which work has recently resumed, and on October 5, 1981, he opened Madinat al-Salam (City of Peace). These projects were close to his heart—he would place the first brick, plant the first tree, open the first building. Once Lulee teased him by saying that she had missed the soap operas on television for three days in a row because they had been interrupted by coverage of Father performing various activities for the new cities. "I know, isn't it boring?" he agreed. "I told them it was too much for everyone to have to watch me so often."

In 1978 he instituted an arts and culture festival, which was to be held annually on October 8. It followed the military celebration of the October War on October 6. The arts and culture festival started in the evening with a party attended by all the members of government and people in show business. Before it began, Father would award degrees to chosen entertainers. This ceremony provoked inevitable political jokes about the distinction that was being conferred upon humble singers and actors, but their joy was obvious and touching. One of the people honored was Mohammed Abdel

Wahab, an old man by this time, whose "modern" melodies had been current during the first half of the century and who is still a major influence on popular music. Father also asked the movie industry to stop making war movies—they had been making them for as long as I could remember. They stopped and, instead, produced films that focused on Egyptian history and culture. There was a miniseries on television that dealt with the 1952 revolution with a complete lack of censorship. I watched part of it with Father, who explained who everyone was and the political background. There were also several series that dealt with cultural issues, the tribulations of a Muslim father, for instance, who had to raise four motherless daughters. At the festival Father spoke to an actor in one of these cultural movies. "You made me cry the other day when I saw your film. You must do that again."

•

After his successes at Camp David, Father began to make some perceptible changes in his behavior toward me. Later, I noticed that he also paid more attention to my sisters and to his grandchildren from his first marriage. It was as though Camp David and the Nobel Peace Prize together represented to him a pinnacle in his public life. Now, it seemed he was prepared to focus his energies on rediscovering his entire family and his roots in his beloved rural Egypt. As I look back, I can see that events seemed to fall into a new pattern, as Father became more attentive, more solicitous, and more loving. Tragically, I viewed the changes as though at a great distance. It is not that I was not touched or that I was not grateful. The problem was that I felt things had gone too far for an easy rapprochement to be accomplished. I credit Father for doing his best, however.

During these years I still worked for Hoechst pharmaceuticals. Officials in Germany invited me to visit them there in 1974. Before I left Egypt, I was expected as a courtesy to seek Father's approval as head of the family. Father arranged in 1974 for Rawia and me to have diplomatic passports, as his second family did. Father's behavior had alternated between indifference and indulgence for many years now and I longed for him to be consistent.

In December, before I left for Germany, Father called me. He dropped broad hints about the things he wanted me to bring back to

1975. Dressed up for a carnival, my resemblance to Father is striking, and very comical!

December 1975. With my second husband, Nader, and Rokaya on our wedding day.

January 1978. Gamal's wedding. From right to left, Lulee, Gamal, Dina, and me.

1980. With the Chinese ambassador.

Aswan, December 1980. Father meets the chief executives of Hoechst pharmaceuticals, where I worked.

After my father's death, Jihan gave me this picture and wrote on it, "To lovely Camelia, my best wishes and good luck. Jihan Anwar Sadat."

Father gave me this photo in 1979 and wrote on it, "To my daughter Camelia with blessings, Anwar Sadat."

Father reading the Koran during Ramadan. He would tape the recitation for his family. (Konrad R. Müller)

The low *tableia* set for a meal. (Konrad R. Müller)

Father in the traditional galabia on the veranda. (Konrad R. Müller)

Father taking his morning walk in the garden of his house in the village. (Konrad R. Müller)

Father with Lulee and me in July 1981. It is the last picture I have of him.

Father, minutes before his assassination, was watching a display of jets.

(From left) Rawia, little Jihan, and I.

Embracing Jihan at the forty-day ceremony after Father's funeral.

At father's grave.

Jihan, little Jihan, and Mother in July 1984.

Receiving my M.A. from Dean Bernard Redmont at Boston University in May 1983.

Boston, April 1985. A brief hand-shake with Jimmy Carter during the promotion of his recent book. (Perry's Studio).

Lulee and I in 1985.

him. He adored white chocolate and Velamints, and I usually brought other gifts, such as cufflinks, ties, or a pipe for him as well. When I returned, Father would act like a small child peering eagerly into the bags I produced, his face lit with anticipation.

After my trip I called him, and he asked me to come and visit him, since, he said, no one would be at home with him that weekend and he wanted to talk. This was my first indication that Father had changed his behavior toward me. I found that he had also increased his socializing with Rokaya and Rawia, and he began to see his grandchildren by his first three daughters. Until that time, Lulee had rarely met her grandfather, but now she blossomed with his attention. Father would ask his grandchildren about their progress in school, their everyday difficulties. He would hand out small gifts and mementoes from his attaché case—I still have a pen he used to sign the Camp David accords.

He bought cars for Rokaya's son Mohammed and for one of Rawia's sons, another Mohammed, when they graduated from high school. He promised the same for Rokaya's and Rawia's other two sons when they graduated. His grandaughters were younger and, instead, he counseled them about their grooming, their hairstyles, dress, and perfume. He made them feel appreciated as young women. One day he looked at my twelve-year-old-daughter, Lulee, and said to me, "When you were twelve you used to drive me crazy, but now you are so mature and lovely." He looked at Lulee again. "She is becoming such a beautiful woman, Camelia. You will be a mother-in-law and a grandmother sooner than you think," he joked.

In 1979 Father was awarded the Nobel Peace Prize with Menachem Begin. He donated his share of the prize money to the modernization of Mit Abul-Kum along with the royalty earnings from his autobiography, *In Search of Identity*, which he wrote in 1978.

In February 1980 Father put himself out particularly for me. On my trip to the Hoechst headquarters in Germany I had met a member of the company who had cancer. He had told me that before he died he hoped to meet Anwar el-Sadat.

"Fine. I will receive him if he comes here," Father replied when I told him. I was a bit incredulous, and said, "Look, Father, don't be polite. Don't say you will meet him if you will not. They might fire me if I fouled up," I teased. "You don't want to get your daughter fired, do you?"

"No! You can count on me," Father assured me. In the past, Father would not have suggested such a thing for me or for my colleagues.

The German arrived with some other Hoechst officials and I called Father's office to confirm the meeting. An officer answered the phone and told me Father had gone to Aswan. My heart sank, but I was outwardly calm. I asked the officer to call Aswan and remind Father of his appointment with the German visitors. Shortly afterward, the officer called and informed me most respectfully that my father expected us, and that if we went to the presidential VIP lounge at the airport, we would be met, and flown by Father's plane to Aswan.

When we arrived in Aswan, I was told that, because he had to complete a meeting with government officials, Father could not be available at the appointed time. However, he sent his apologies and said he would be with us soon. When Father arrived, he embraced and kissed me. As in the old days, I kissed his hand as a sign of respect. His warmth and hospitality impressed the Germans enormously. The next day, photographs of Father and me with the German visitors appeared on the front pages of Egyptian newspapers. It was the first time I ever had been in a published photo with my father.

An amusing incident at that time showed how much of an unknown I remained in the eyes of the Egyptian press. Father had invited me to his beach house outside Alexandria. He also expected Gaafar al-Nimeiry, the Sudanese head of state, who usually vacationed at the beach in Egypt. Being behind schedule, Father asked me to join him in going to the airport to meet Nimeiry. He led me to the car, holding my hand. Television reporters who trailed Father began photographing us as we went to his Rolls-Royce and continued after we drove away. Next day, the television carried pictures of Father walking and holding hands with me and footage of us sitting side-by-side in the car. Gossip followed that Father was involved with an attractive young woman whom he intended to marry. I thought it a huge joke, since I was the woman they meant.

Father's Rolls-Royce brought out some of his childlike qualities. The manufacturer had given him the car. He accepted it for his use, but made it clear that he considered it government property, rather than his own. He never would let a chauffeur drive that Rolls on the road. When it went out, as on the day Nimeiry arrived, Father himself was at the wheel.

During my visit to his beach house in Alexandria Father also showed exasperation with bureaucracy in Egypt. He told me that two years earlier, a foreign government had given him a check for about a million dollars to establish a poultry and egg production center as part of the Egyptian development program. Father suggested that the outskirts of Alexandria would be a good location. Two years later, he remembered the project and wondered what had happened. "You know, Camelia, they told me that because the check had been made out to me, they never cashed it. Can you believe that? All the jobs it would have created, the whole project lost because no one thought to ask me to endorse that check!"

Later, in the spring, I went to visit him. It was two days after the Shah of Iran had died, and I told him that I admired his steadfast friendship with the Shah, who had been abandoned by everybody, including the U.S. government. Father had given him refuge in Egypt after he had been deposed by the revolution in Iran in 1979, and when he died Father gave him a military funeral. Now, two days later, Father complained that his feet were still blistered from the four-mile funeral procession, which he had walked in his heavy military boots.

In the summer of 1980 Rawia told me that she was going to Father's beach house in Alexandria and asked me to accompany her. We arrived in the heat of the afternoon to find Father reading in the garden, scorning, as usual, the benefits of the air-conditioning inside. After greeting us and talking for an hour or so, he asked us to excuse him while he took a nap. We immediately said that we would leave, but he insisted that we stay and have dinner with him. "We'll eat in an hour and I'd like you to stay, since your stepmother and the children are out of the country and I am alone," he said.

We went to rest, and he ordered water and fruit to be brought to our rooms. Over four hours passed and Rawia and I became concerned about our father—we had never known him to take a nap before. Eventually we were told that Father was waiting for us in the dining room. "I am sorry, my children," he apologized. "I have never been tired like this before. I have taken up the time you spent to see me with sleeping." He continued to apologize throughout the meal. Afterward, though we protested, he pressed us to stay the night to keep him company.

"But we don't have night clothes," we countered.

"That's no problem. You can use my pajama jackets. I'll wake you up early and we can have breakfast together."

We accepted. After dinner, we went to the basement and watched an old film with Father. He took us each to our rooms, checked to see that we had enough fruit, and kissed us good night. Rawia and I could hardly believe the care our father was lavishing on us. We felt as though we were ten and twelve again and living in his house as his children. Neither of us slept that night. We stayed up and talked of all our memories of Father. The next morning we had breakfast, and Father walked us to the door and gave each of us an envelope containing money. We were driven back in Father's new Mercedes, escorted by a police car.

When I got into the car and it started moving, I turned to Rawia and told her that if things were going to change again, if Father was going to revert to his former indifference, I wanted to die right then, at that moment, filled with the memory of our visit.

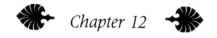 *Chapter 12*

MIT ABUL–KUM REVISITED

THERE ARE two roads from Cairo to Mit Abul-Kum. One is the main northern highway to Alexandria, which you take as far as Quisna and then plunge west on to a narrow road that takes you to the village. The route I prefer, however, starts west of Cairo and winds sleepily through the many small villages in the Nile Delta. In the summer, the trees that line each side of it meet overhead to form a cool canopy of leaves. The fields are filled with summer citrus trees, their dark green leaves a glossy foil to the bright orange and lemon fruit and golden blossoms, and the air is fragrant with their fresh, strong scent.

The biggest town before Mit Abul-Kum is Shebein el-Kum. About ten miles farther on you can see a cluster of high buildings on the river. Their six- or seven-story height makes them conspicuously modern after the other villages; it is the first sign of the modernized Mit Abul-Kum. A hundred yards before the village, on the right, is the Sadat family cemetery, encircled by a white fence and closed with two large steel gates. One side is reserved for women, the other side is for men and includes the grave of my uncle 'Atif, who was killed in the October War. After the cemetery on the left is Father's house, and opposite, down a small street, is the Madi house, where my mother was born. It was later split into six dwellings, and Mohammed Madi, the *omda* of Mit Abul-Kum, and his brothers lived there.

Farther along the main road, beyond Father's house, is the house my father had built for his father in the 1960s, where Mohammed el-Sadat lived until his death in 1972. Next to Grandfather's house is Nafeisa's house, then that of Esmat—Father's sister and brother. Once my father showed me a piece of land. "I'm going to build houses for you and your sisters," he declared. I was thrilled at the time, and one day I still hope to build a house in Mit Abul-Kum.

If I love Mit Abul-Kum for all the ways it has enriched my life, my feelings for the village could be only a fraction of what Father felt. Mit Abul-Kum was one of his main sources of strength as he faced life's adversities and as he focused his mental and physical powers for his moments of greatness. His increasing visits to the village in the post–Camp David period served as a reaffirmation of his psychological bonds with our ancient land and its most basic values. They also provided opportunities for him to reaffirm his relationship with his rather traditional first family, his rural kin, and the plain people of Egypt, whom he cherished.

Mit Abul-Kum is part of the Menofeia governorate, one of the more affluent in Egypt. After the revolution in 1952 there was limited agrarian reform and each of the *fellahin* who worked on the land was given five *fedans* of land (over 4½ acres) that previously belonged to the landowner. Under Nasser, the Menofeia governorate had been granted funds to pave the dusty roads. With the money from the Nobel Peace Prize and his royalties from *In Search of Identity*, Father modernized his village. He called it the "New Mit Abul-Kum." The villagers even had color TV before I did in Cairo.

On one of my visits, he had asked me to come to see the new brick houses. While he was looking at them, villagers came up and started complaining about how there was not enough space in the new houses and how they had wanted this house and not the other. Father put his hand on their shoulders and nodded at the engineer who was with him. "Take note of all this," he said to the engineer. "These people are going to be living here forever and I want them to live in comfort. I want them to have houses they can use." The houses also used the innovative solar energy panels. Father's technological adviser, Farouk el-Baz, had told him about them and he was proud that he had used them in Mit Abul-Kum.

Father had spoken to me about his decision to modernize the village. Apparently, his other children thought he should have given them his royalties. "I could have split the money between you all," he explained. "But this money would spoil your lives. I, myself, wouldn't know what to do with such a large amount of money," he added, playing his role as a poor *fellah* from the village. (Unfortunately, the Egyptian government has not understood the situation at all. In 1985 the tax department sent me, as one of Sadat's inheritors, a bill for 58,499 Egyptian pounds for taxes on his royalty earnings.) "Mit Abul-Kum will be a modern village," he went on, "with new houses and good sanitation and no disease." And it happened—they burned the very poor part of the village first and the most destitute villagers were the first to move into the new houses.

It was this visit that finally convinced me that Father's change of behavior was a permanent thing and that in a personal way he had moved on to a very spiritual way of perceiving things. Our conversation about family matters was intimate and frank, and yet he was also joking and laughing with me as if he were talking to a good friend. I felt that I had come home. I remembered when my sisters and I had asked him if we were his children and he had replied that he thought of us as sisters. Now, it seemed I had found the best of both worlds—I had his love, and he shared his thoughts with me.

.

Because his second family often had other things to do, Father would often invite Rokaya, Rawia, and me down to see him in the village. In July 1980, he invited us to spend a day at the end of Ramadan with him. The rising of the new crescent moon signals the end of the lunar month of Ramadan, when Muslims fast during the daylight hours, and Father would always be in Mit Abul-Kum for the second half of the month.

We arrived at night and ate "breakfast," the first meal after sundown, with Father. He ate his customary spoonful of honey and fruit salts to start his digestion before eating properly an hour later. When Father became president, he had given up eating at the low, old-fashioned *tableia*, or dining table. Now, however, he started using it again, and in the village, he would often eat with his hands instead of with Western knives, forks, and spoons. It seemed clear that he was returning to his rural roots.

"My children," he said as we sat down to eat that evening, "I shall need you to stay tomorrow night as well. I am going to give a wedding party for Aisha and I would like you to entertain our guests." Aisha was one of his sister Nafeisa's nine children. She was going to marry an army officer whose father was a clerk in the presidential offices.

Because we had been brought up to observe the traditional courtesies, such as not smoking or crossing one's legs in front of older people, and we kissed his hand in the old way, Father loved to have my sisters and me at formal occasions when he would proudly introduce us to his relatives.

After dinner we talked, the candlelight throwing deep shadows on our faces. We relaxed in the soothing silence of the village, after the restless bustle of Cairo. Outside, the vast night sky was filled with stars.

The next morning, Father awoke early and prayed in the mosque with the village men. Then he returned and, picking up his stick, he went out for his half-hour morning walk wearing comfortable sports clothes—shorts, T-shirt, and running shoes. After his walk he would have a massage or use an exercise bicycle. In the evening he would walk or jog for a further hour. Even when he was not fasting, Father would typically skip lunch, and for dinner he would eat vegetables with chicken, although he also loved spaghetti.

Father always took care to dress well and comfortably. He would wear a galabia in the village when he did not have to meet anyone. The only time he would wear a galabia in public was for his annual television interview on his birthday, December 25, when he would talk about the village customs. Otherwise he would wear light cotton safari suits with long sleeves. One day he was named one of the ten best-dressed men in the world by a prestigious Italian clothing manufacturer. Father was obviously delighted. "Can you believe, Camelia, that this *fellah* from Mit Abul-Kum would ever receive such recognition?" he crowed delightedly. I was amused—I could not recall that he had been *this* delighted when he had received the Nobel Prize. All his galabias and suits were made by the faithful Swalim, who was his tailor for more than thirty years and made clothes for all the men in our family.

At noon on that July morning, Father held a press conference with a foreign correspondent. It was not uncommon during those years for him to arrange even for foreign dignitaries to visit him in the village. He would fly them out by helicopter. I watched Father being interviewed with pleasure as I saw him laugh and characteristically hesitate, uttering a soft "ah . . . ah . . ." as he sought the right word. I loved hearing my father talk. His voice was deep and melodious and he had a great command of classical Arabic. His pronunciation shaped each word into its precise form and gave a simple elegance to his speech.

In the afternoon, Father recited prayers from the Koran until sunset. He would read through the Koran completely over the course of Ramadan.

After sundown, we attended the wedding breakfast for the newly married couple. I could see that the groom's family were thrilled and not a little awed by having the president act as host and the president's daughters serve them with candy and cakes.

Father was always thoughtful toward his relatives. Some of them lived in the poor parts of Cairo, and during Ramadan Father would hire a bus so that they could come to the village to share breakfast. He also gave them money for their pilgrimages to Mecca. But the thing that gave them the most joy was that the press would take photographs of him with them, and the next day they would see pictures of the president entertaining his relatives in the newspapers or on TV.

By this time, Father had also taken on the unofficial role of *omda*, or mayor, of Mit Abul-Kum. My mother's brother Mohammed Madi died in 1979. He had been *omda* since 1911 but afterward no new *omda* was appointed. Father helped all the villagers, not only his relatives. He listened to their problems and resolved disputes. When the teacher of El Kottab died, he went by helicopter to the funeral and afterward spoke with the villagers, holding them familiarly by their shoulders.

The next day was the first of three feast days that celebrate the end of Ramadan. It is called Id al-Fitr, and in the morning there are traditional prayers in the mosque at dawn. During the day people visit one another and exchange gifts of money and eat an assortment of cookies called *kahk*. Father never spent this day in the village, although it was customary to celebrate it with one's family. On that day, he would always visit "his children," meaning Egyptian citizens in the armed forces who were on active duty and would travel to various places where they were stationed to be with them.

That evening, I went to my room, feeling strengthened by my contact with Father and the village. As I drifted off to sleep, I remembered the satellite picture of Egypt that President Carter had

given Father, much to his delight and astonishment. Mit Abul-Kum
was recognizably there, visible from all those miles in space.

I still intended to leave Egypt. In some ways, that decision had
made this period of reconciliation much sweeter; I was calm in my
resolve. Unintentionally, Father had boosted my courage. I was talking to him one day in 1979 about his determination to solve the
problems between Egypt and Israel. He spoke in general terms:
"We are a product of our past, but we cannot be chained down by
it. We have to decide, both morally and objectively, what is right.
Then we must act upon what we have decided."

There were still things that I wanted to discuss with Father, but I
did not want to damage our newfound relationship, and I knew that
these were things that I needed to work out at a distance. For the
second time, the thought of writing him a letter occurred to me. I
thought I could write it and then, perhaps, I would not need to send
it to him.

In Cairo, I became something of a recluse. After my argument
with Fawzi Abdel Hafez over Nader and his effect on how people
might think of me, I cut myself off socially. I jogged and swam and I
watched a lot of soccer. I had been an avid soccer fan since 1960,
and I would often go to support my team (Zamalek, one of the Cairo
teams), in the cheapest seats, jumping up excitedly when the team
scored.

My first thoughts were of a life in Germany. I believed I could get
a job in Hoechst pharmaceuticals there. Since I worked for Hoechst
in Egypt, I knew the people at the European headquarters. Also,
having been educated at the German School in Cairo, I spoke German fluently and knew the culture of the country. I could study for
an advanced degree, since there are graduate communications programs in Germany. Hoechst itself offered a program, but I found it
did not terminate in a degree. Then I talked with a friend, who
suggested that I go to the United States, where there are numerous
graduate programs in my field.

I had never been to the United States. At best, I had a functional
command of English. I had taken a three-month course at the
Berlitz language school in Cairo and had a feeling for English gram-

mar. There also would be the problem of Lulee's adaptation to school in the United States, but Lulee attended the English School in Cairo, and virtually all her classes were conducted in English.

•

In December 1980, during the Iranian hostage crisis, I made a trip to the States to scout different schools. I spent my first day in New York. I found the scale of the city and the activity to be overwhelming—actually frightening—after my more-or-less suburban life in Cairo. Compared to warm days in Cairo, the cold chilled me all the way through. I hope nothing freezes and falls off, I thought as I pulled my coat tight around me.

Later, I arrived in Chicago. It seemed colder still, and the hugeness of the city became oppressive. I made a short hop via air to Minneapolis. Up till I arrived in the Twin Cities airport, I thought I understood about cold weather from Germany, New York, and Chicago. In Minneapolis I still had something to learn about being frozen alive. The wind caused tears to roll down my cheeks. My body heat could barely keep the water from freezing on my cheeks. Could I ever survive in the upper Midwest of the United States? Doubtful, I muttered.

I came to Massachusetts to visit a friend in Worcester, which is west of Boston. Elaine Saliba, whose family originated in Lebanon, is someone I met through a friend in Cairo. "How about considering a university in Boston?" Elaine suggested. She mentioned Boston University's School of Public Communication. I visited B.U. one day. I liked what I found, overall. The next day I made my formal application, signing my name, Camelia Sadat. The way I was treated, one might think a Sadat signed up at least once a day at the university. Then Elaine took me to meet Dr. Michael Massouh, a vice-president at the university, who is also of Lebanese extraction. That visit reinforced my image of Boston as a friendly place to study.

I got a tour of Boston. I found it enchanting—very European in atmosphere. Somehow, the weather seemed less cold than in New York, Chicago, and Minneapolis. The weather reminded me of winter in England. I can deal with that, I decided.

When Elaine and her children picked me up to take me to the airport, her children were hungry. "Do you mind if we stop for something to eat?" she asked. "Not at all," I said. She drove into the parking lot of a Burger King restaurant. In Egypt, we have a burger chain called Wimpy's, so, of course, I was familiar with hamburgers. However, when I saw my first Whopper, I was astounded. First, the hugeness of it. Then, I looked at the thickness of the meat patty. And I took in the "extras"—lettuce, tomato, onions, mustard, and sesame-seed bun. It looked like a fantastic Wimpy's burger fused with a salad. And the flavor. That was something else.

After munching through my Whopper, I asked Elaine, "Do you think I could have another?"

"Sure." She smiled. "Maybe we should get you three or four, so that you will not starve on your flight to London tonight."

Upon leaving Boston, I caught my flight to London, where I would spend the Christmas holiday. From there, I called Father by phone to greet him on his birthday.

Later, my sisters, who had been with Father to celebrate his birthday, said he appeared distracted till he got my call. Then he became animated. When I told him I had purchased a Dunhill pipe, a tie, and other gifts for him, he really perked up. I think he felt sincerely happy to get my call, since we had been getting along quite well recently.

Father knew I had been to the States to inspect graduate schools, so that was no surprise to him. In the call from London, I informed him I had made an application at Boston University. "We will talk about it when I get home," I said.

"When will you be back?" Father inquired.

"On December thirty-first," I replied.

"We will get together then," he said. I did not even have to ask for an appointment.

In Cairo, I met with my father while reporters, photographers, and television cameramen surrounded him. I think he had been in the midst of a press conference. As I approached, he leaned toward me and whispered, "What do you have there for me?" He meant the gifts bought for him on my trip.

He totally forgot the people around him. He acted as though he wished they would just vanish while he got down to examining the "precious" gifts I had for him. Father's enthusiasm for my gifts thrilled me, and it made me even happier when I saw him on television wearing the ties I had given him.

Later, Father and I talked about my trip to the States. He professed pride that I planned to enter a graduate program after I completed my studies at Cairo University. "You will be the first of my children to earn a graduate degree," he said.

His demeanor suggested that while he supported the idea of my studying for a master's degree, he hoped I would not leave Egypt. After he had rediscovered his first family and grandchildren, following Camp David, it would be hard for him to see Lulee and me leave for a foreign country. As a traditional Muslim, my father seemed to feel he had the responsibility to watch over his family, especially the females. He might have felt, too, that we were in danger due to the fierce opposition to his peace initiative with Israel.

Father had received word from Boston University president John Silber, through the Egyptian embassy in Washington, that I had gained admission at B.U. Dr. Silber commented that the university had many international students, including some Arabs who opposed Father's policy of moderation in the Middle East. There also had been some incidents there after the Iranians released their American hostages. There would be concern for the safety of someone named Sadat, he suggested.

So my father, whose full name was Mohammed Anwar Mohammed el-Sadat, wanted to discuss the situation.

"Camelia, my daughter," he said with doleful eyes, "you will be giving up your name, your job, your lovely home—everything—to go to the States. Here you have a university, too. Here you could have everything. In America you won't be safe. Some fanatic may discover you are my daughter and use you as a target."

Father, the master negotiator, was at it again. But I would not back down. "Father, we have discussed that before, and you know my feelings," I said.

We discussed the problem of security. Finally we agreed to drop the family name Sadat and retain the name of my father's father, Mohammed. "Well, you have lost my last name," I remember Father saying. "But how long can you fool people? You still have my face."

"No need to worry." I smiled. "I am much prettier than you."

Later, just before we left Cairo for Boston, Father met Lulee and me. As a father he really did not want me to move to the States, but he was too proud to beg or command. Father looked at me with his dark, sad eyes and said "This might be the last time you see me alive."

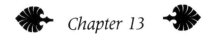 *Chapter 13*

A NEW WORLD IN BOSTON

ON AN AUGUST DAY IN 1981 I awoke in a Boston motel in a stupor after a fitful four-hour sleep. Before retiring, my daughter, Lulee, and I had completed a twenty-six-hour trip by air from Cairo, which was enough to stun anyone. Fingers of daylight had begun to probe into the room. I knew I had to get organized to face my first day at Boston University.

After a while I called Dr. Michael Massouh, the vice-president whom I had met on my visit in January. "Good morning. This is Camelia Sa—Camelia Mohammed," I said to him. It was the first time I used this name. Dr. Massouh was one of the few people in the university who knew my true identity. He said he would send a man to the motel to help us move our luggage to a temporary apartment on Commonwealth Avenue, at the heart of the campus.

It was 12:30 P.M. when the man lugged the valise of my fifteen-year-old daughter up the steps to a pretty brownstone. He left us with a big trunk that weighed about 150 pounds. I looked at Lulee, and she looked at me. We shrugged and hoisted the trunk from either end.

Three floors later we caught our breath and silently viewed the bare rooms. We found three beds—nothing more. Lulee had reluctantly agreed to accompany me to the States "just to test it out." From the look on her face it was obvious that she already had her doubts.

We sat on the floor and drank cold Cokes, then I went downstairs to telephone my friend Elaine Saliba. Elaine had offered to help me get settled when I moved. I told her I needed to buy some necessities. "I will come and pick you up in a little while," she said. "I know a place that is having a sale." Elaine arrived about an hour later, and she and I went to a major department store. Soon we were carrying my purchases to the cashier. I had six pillows, three blankets, six sets of sheets, an assortment of bath towels, and some glasses and plates. The sales clerk rang them up and told me the total. It came to $1,500. If this is typical of prices in the United States, I thought, I do not know if we will survive. In Europe the same purchases would have cost me much less, especially on sale. As we drove home, I added figures aloud in Arabic.

"What did you say?" Elaine asked.

"I was just wondering how I can afford to buy all the things we will need, like furniture and a car."

During the next few days, with Elaine's help I went to several rental places and picked out tables and chairs and bureaus. At the end of the week, I called Rawia back home in Cairo and asked her to mail me some of my savings. The fund transfer came just in time because we desperately needed appliances.

I contemplated another shopping trip, and a friend of Elaine's suggested a discount store. The next day Lulee and I went on our first independent hunt for bargains across town. It was also Lulee's first ride on a Boston trolley. She had been put off by public buses in Cairo, which are usually jam-packed. Riders are not only crammed on the inside but sometimes also hang out of the doors and even perch on the roof. When we got on the first trolley we could not find a seat, but there was standing room. Lulee had a gleam in her eyes—until the car lunged and she fell to the floor. She scrambled to her feet, unhurt. Then she asked when we would get a car.

At the discount store we had a great time shopping for our apartment. At the checkout, a saleswoman asked our nationality. Egyptian, I replied. "Oh," she said, "you know, my dream is to visit Egypt to see President Sadat and the Pyramids!"

"Pretty good," I said to Lulee in Arabic. "Your grandfather is one step ahead of the Pyramids!"

For the next couple of days Lulee and I practically lived in the local supermarket. It was cool, close by, and best of all, stocked with familiar foods. The supermarket was a novelty, because in Egypt there are many separate butchers, bakers, and vegetable vendors. Each store sells only a few items, and each always has a long line with rich and poor people alike. Because most food is in short supply, the government must ration it. The food is cheap if you can find what you want. Our family in the village often helped supplement what we found in Cairo for our household larders.

Unfortunately, we could not find kosher-style meat in our Boston supermarket. Muslims are supposed to eat meat prepared in the kosher manner. There are supposed to be a lot of Jewish people in Boston, and I was surprised that they did not all eat kosher meat. Those who did had to get it at special butcher shops.

The bank was not far from the market—a real convenience. In Egypt I had to drive the crowded streets into town during bank hours to cash my checks. Another problem was that in Arabic, the characters are very precise, and if you change your signature slightly, which I often did, your check would not be accepted. Here, I opened an account with no problem. When I stopped at the bank one day in mid-August, one of the officers, a conservatively dressed man, studied a form I filled out and then stared at me. Finally, he said, "Pardon me, miss, are you Egyptian?"

"Yes. . ."

"I am a great admirer of your president. Have you seen him? Sadat is more than a great leader. He is an international symbol of hope, more than anyone of our time."

I fought off an urge to blurt out my name. I said thank you and walked into the sunshine. It was wonderful to know that my father was cared for by so many people so far from home. In fact, in Europe, where he was respected as a man of peace, I did not sense such strong admiration. It seemed strange that under these circumstances I had to change my name for security reasons.

That night Lulee and I were watching TV. The news came on at 11:00 P.M. I was dozing when Lulee shouted, "Look, there is grandfather!"

I opened my eyes and saw Father hugging President Reagan at the White House.

"Mommy, did you know he was coming so soon?"

"I did not expect him for weeks."

"Can we see him?"

"No, they said he has already left for Egypt," I said.

"Do you think he tried to call?"

"How could he?" I said to Lulee. "We do not even have a phone yet."

"Do you think he looked tired?"

I kissed Lulee and told her to go to bed. "Do not worry, Lulee, he will be back again soon. Meanwhile, we will call home when the phone is connected." I lay awake that night thinking about Lulee's last question to me. What troubled me was that my father looked so thin, so unlike himself. For the next week or so I did not think too much about my father during the day. I was too busy running around and tending to my own life. I found that everything consumed much of my time since I did not yet know in which areas or stores I could find what I needed to buy.

August 12, 1981, came and it was a day set aside for school, Lulee's and mine. As I walked down Commonwealth Avenue on my way to the School of Public Communication at Boston University, it was a bright, clear day, and people were in good spirits. Across the street a row of brownstones were covered with ivy, and colorful plants dotted the balconies. I passed a sidewalk café dwarfed by a high-rise dormitory. In a way, the blend of old and new made me feel at home.

As I approached the communications school, my stomach began to churn. I was a thirty-two-year-old student/mother who felt like a little girl on her first day of school. I was anxious in part because I was about to see the dean, Mrs. Doris Dondis. When I had seen her in January she was discouraging about everything and almost scared me out of her office. Later, much to my surprise, she greeted me like an old friend. She took me on a tour of the building and introduced me to people with whom I would be dealing. Then we went back to her office, where we chose my courses. This system was new to me. At Cairo University the professors did not get so close to the students, because the students were automatically assigned to classes. I liked the freedom here.

After a long discussion Dean Dondis walked outside with me. On the way we passed the school auditorium. "You have probably never seen such a large classroom before," she said. "This holds two hundred students!" I was about to tell her about Cairo's lecture halls, which hold three thousand students. Some Americans seem convinced that a country like Egypt lags in everything, as compared with the United States.

Back at the apartment in mid-afternoon I found Lulee sitting on the couch eating pretzels and watching *The Guiding Light*. She was so engrossed with the show that she did not answer my greeting. "Come on, Lulee, you are spending too much time with the TV."

"But, Mommy, it is just like *Dallas*." She knew I looked forward to the soaps in the evening, so it was hard to argue with her.

"Anyway, Lulee, we have to go register you at the high school," I said.

Although she had studied in Cairo's English School Lulee was anxious about whether she could keep up with American English in the classroom. She was also nervous about meeting so many new people. I could appreciate how she felt because we shared many of the same fears.

When we reached the front door of Lulee's high school in Brookline I said, "I am sure you will like it." To our surprise the door was locked. We tried the doors on the side of the building, but they too were locked.

Finally a young girl came up to us and introduced herself, "Classes are not in session during the summer, but the offices are open. My name is Daphna, by the way." She led us to the back door and then took us to the main office. While we signed the necessary forms, she waited. Then she accompanied us back to the trolley stop, chatting with Lulee as though they were sisters.

"So you're from Egypt," Daphna said. "That's interesting. You're the first people I've ever met from Egypt."

"Really? Where are you from?"

"Israel."

Leave the irony to the historians, I thought. Left alone, tenth graders might solve all the problems. I looked at them and thought, Lulee will be very lucky if everyone is this nice. As it turned out, Daphna became her best and only friend for a while.

·

The following evening Lulee and I were watching TV when the phone rang. It was Elaine. She wanted to know how I was feeling, but the urgency in her voice suggested that she had another reason for calling.

"Camelia, did you hear what happened?"

"No," I responded. "What?"

"There was a big political crackdown in Egypt. Your father has arrested thousands of people."

"Arrested? Who? Was there violence?"

"I am not sure. It has something to do with the Peace Treaty. They said that certain people had been threatening . . ."

I knew about the "certain people." Prior to the Camp David meetings Father had informed President Carter of a planned democratization of Egypt. Because the political lid had been clamped down tightly in Egypt for so long, when the liberalization got under way people of all persuasions sprang forth to demand changes reflecting their vested interests. Some might be called Islamic fanatics. But others were members of the Muslim Brotherhood, and there were also Coptic Christians, judges, lawyers, and journalists. Some demanded a continuing war with Israel on religious grounds, and others strenuously opposed the Camp David accords for various reasons. Still others advocated Egyptian supremacy over other governments in the region.

The Ministry of the Interior's security force reported rumors of a coup. Father feared that instead of moving toward democracy, Egypt was fast sliding toward anarchy. Consequently he ordered about 1,500 put in jail.

I earnestly believe Father felt the state faced destruction. I do not think he feared for his political future but for that of Egypt. Father had already told President Carter of his intention to resign the presidency in 1982, so it could not be said that he intended to perpetuate himself in power. Also, he had an unusual tolerance for opposing views.

For example, during the Nasser period, the influential Wafd political party and all other parties were abolished in 1954, because of alleged corruption. In 1960 the Nasser regime allowed the formation of one party, the Arab Socialist Union. After Father became Nasser's successor, he approved a plan in 1974 to begin the democratization of Egypt, and set up procedures for the recognition of political parties. By 1977 three fledgling political parties had been recognized—one socialist, one communist, and one opposition party. By the time of Camp David, the three parties were taking positions. Father suffered a lot of attacks, many of them highly personal and offensive, rather than criticism focused on issues and agendas.

"Have you seen this?" I asked one day in regard to a newspaper article that impugned my father. "How can you allow this? They are attacking you personally, hurting you!" This was one of very few times that I had a political discussion with Father. The treatment that he got from the opposition was unfair, even outrageous, I felt. Surprisingly, my father viewed the situation with amusement rather than sharing my rage.

"You have to realize, Camelia, that they have not been allowed to talk freely about politics for years," he told me. "It is as though a man has been locked for years in an unlighted room, and then someone opens the door." Father continued, "When the door opens even a little, the man sees the light and begins running. He would hurt or smash anyone to get out into the light. He runs and keeps on running. He has no sense of direction. Only after he gets tired does he begin thinking about the direction he should take. When he does decide, he could be wrong. Or, if he is lucky, the direction could result in something good.

"That is what democracy is about, Camelia," Father said, looking at me wistfully. "It is the right to be free and to choose—even if it is the wrong choice. Unfortunately, I am the target at the present time. However, there is no quick solution. I tend to think of myself as a builder who goes from place to place to make foundations for structures that are needed. They will rise eventually. It takes patience."

"How long?" I asked.

"Probably not in my lifetime," he told me. "Maybe in fifty years."

I did not understand that kind of patience under the existing conditions, but it was my father's way.

"The competition of ideas and programs will eventually result in a better life for Egypt," Father went on. "We must gain confidence in the people. Power must reside in the people—not in the old political centers of influence," he said. "Do not keep thinking of this as an attack on me, personally," Father concluded.

That did not keep me from worrying that some of Father's opponents were fanatics who believed assassination to be a legitimate solution to their political frustrations. Yet today as I look at the evolution of the political party structure and the emergence of the New Wafd party, I can see Father's trust in Egyptians and his belief in the evolution of the democratic process being upheld.

After Elaine's call I dialed the overseas operator. She put me through to my father's country home, where we had shared so many special times. I thought he might have retreated there to be by himself. I figured that now was a good time to reach him. It was 7:30 P.M. in Egypt. One of Father's servants answered. I told him who was calling. He asked me to wait and said he would inform the president that I was on the line. Moments later, the servant returned to inform me that the president was resting and did not want to be disturbed. When I hung up Lulee took my hand and asked me what was wrong.

"I do not know, Lulee."

"Why can we not reach Grandfather? We have not heard his voice since . . ." Her voice trailed off.

•

One of my first classes was in writing. What made this writing class unique was that it was exclusively for international students. The instructor asked everyone to introduce himself and give his nationality. The list unfolded—India, Thailand, the Philippines, Japan, Malaysia, France, Germany, Liberia, Iran, and Egypt. I had been told that Boston University attracted students from all over the world, but I never expected so many nationalities in one room. "Maybe we should rename this class Writing for the United Nations," joked the instructor, a young woman named Nancy Finn. As she spoke, it dawned on me that many of the people I had met in the past two months must have been Jewish. I had not bothered to think about religion one way or the other. But it did strike me as ironic that so many Jewish people here seemed to love Father. Now, in a setting of all international students, I wondered how *they* viewed my father. A while later, during the break, I found out.

There was an Iranian woman who had black eyes and a gaze that I felt could burn a hole though me. She wore a charcoal skirt with a silver belt and a necklace over her blouse, which looked like a plain, white undershirt. On closer inspection, it was clearly a very expensive undershirt. She immediately tried to put me on the defensive—it was as though she instinctively knew my politics. "How do you like what your president did last week?" she asked, raising an eyebrow.

"What do you mean?"

"With his strong-arm tactics, of course." She looked at me intently. "Surely you heard about the purge."

"He had no other choice."

"What? Because people speak out for liberation? Is that grounds for mass arrest?"

"Please! That was not it," I said. "Those people are fanatics who were out to cause trouble. They wanted to turn the country against the Camp David accords."

"How do you know that?"

"I read the papers. They have discovered plots to kill him."

The Iranian was incredulous. "And you believe that propaganda? You really believe everyone is a conspirator?"

"Not everyone."

"That sounds familiar," she said. "I think Sadat is turning out to be just like the Shah. God help you."

I felt a fire raging inside me. But I remained cool. "That is not true. Sadat would never arrest people without a just cause. That is against his nature."

Again, she raised an eyebrow. "Is that so? And how do you know Sadat's nature?"

Since I had arrived in the States, I had felt an almost irresistible urge to reveal my name on several occasions, all of them in response to affectionate remarks. Now, for the first time, I had the same urge for opposing motives. But I would not give the Iranian woman the satisfaction of seeing me display any emotion. Perhaps the university security was right in counseling me to mask my identity, I thought.

·

I had silently feared my first week of school for a long time. It was a challenge unlike any other I had ever faced.

My daughter and I took care of each other. We became students by day and study pals by night. I think that what frustrated us most of all was not the struggle to communicate in English but our failure to communicate with my father.

One thing I could not fit into my schedule was a social life. However, three weeks into the semester, I decided it was time for

Lulee and me to get out. My graduate school was having a picnic, and we went to sample our first American picnic. Actually, the picnic had a largely international flavor because there were many foreign students there. Also, there were numerous professors. But everyone enjoyed the local fare—hamburgers, hot dogs, potato chips, and, of course, beer.

After people felt the effects of a few beers, they began to mingle and kid around—except one of my classmates, who was sitting alone on a bench. It was Lamini Waritay, the Liberian from my writing class. He seemed mysterious from the first time I saw him. His dark glasses blended into his dark face, and it was impossible to see his eyes. As he sat there by himself, I wondered whether he was amused at what he saw or upset. Lulee and I went to talk to him.

"Lamini," I said, "why are you not eating? Can I get you anything?"

He thanked me but said no. Then he offered us seats. "You know," he said, "I have been watching you."

I felt uneasy. "Me? Why?"

"When I first saw you in school I was sure I knew you from somewhere. I could not figure it out until I heard you were from Egypt. Then I saw you speak and the resemblance was unmistakable."

"What do you mean?"

"You introduced yourself in the writing class as Camelia Mohammed. I was sure you would say Sadat. I thought you were his sister. You look just like him, you know."

"You really think so?" I asked matter-of-factly.

"Of course! No one ever told you?"

"No."

Lulee then said something in Arabic. I responded in Arabic, telling her to be quiet so he would not think we were sharing a secret.

"You know," he continued, "I saw Sadat in person in my country. In 1979 he attended the Monrovia Conference [a Liberian peace initiative designed to drum up support for the Camp David accords]. I was a reporter covering the conference, and I remember Sadat's gestures and his mannerisms very well. You have the same bone structure." He pointed to my high, prominent cheekbones.

I looked into his glasses. I still could not see the eyes that apparently did not miss a detail. For a moment no one spoke.

"Oh, do not be silly," said Lulee, breaking the tension. "I have seen lots of pictures of President Sadat. I think my mother is much more beautiful." Lamini laughed for the first time and we joined in happily.

Lulee and I later excused ourselves. As we walked away, I opened my pocketbook. "What are you doing, Mommy?" she asked.

"Just getting a handkerchief," I said. "I feel hot."

"Oh! I was afraid that you were taking out your wallet. I did not think you would want anyone to see the pictures."

I gave Lulee a knowing smile, thinking of the family photos I always carry with me. One picture in particular always amused friends. In it I was dressed in an officer's uniform and hat, and wore a pasted-on mustache. I look so much like a young copy of my father that it is astonishing.

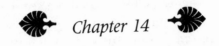

Chapter 14

OCTOBER 6, 1981

OCTOBER 6, 1981, was the anniversary of Egypt's October War against Israel and a day of military celebration in Cairo. In Boston, my daughter had just left for Brookline High School. Then the phone rang. It was my friend Elaine Saliba.

"Camelia," she said anxiously, "did you hear the news?" I thought of the last time she called with news—it was about a political crisis in Egypt. My heart quickened.

"No . . . What is it?"

"Something . . . ," she said, hesitating. Then she continued, "Something happened in the Egyptian army."

"Elaine, what is it? Please tell me." Obviously, she was upset about something that she was reluctant to voice directly. I looked around my cool white Brookline apartment living room with its occasional pieces of Egyptian folk art that I had put up to make the place seem more like home. I waited for her to speak again. Then she said cryptically, "You should call home."

"It is the day of a big military parade, and nobody will be home," I told her. "I will call later."

Elaine tried again. "Camelia," she blurted, "I think you should call *now*. They moved him and the defense minister to the hospital."

"They moved who?"

"Your father."

"My father? What happened?"

"Somebody shot him."

Panic washed over me. My mind pictured my father in the reviewing stand, saluting as his soldiers marched by, caught up in the pageantry of his favorite national holiday—the anniversary of Egypt's successful surprise strike against Israel, which proved his Egypt could bargain for peace from a position of strength. I could see him beaming as thousands of his troops passed by. He was "with his children," so he would not be wearing a bulletproof vest. I called the international operator. "All the lines to Egypt are busy," she reported in that flat voice that phone operators everywhere have.

"Try again!" I pleaded.

After a moment her voice came back, "I am sorry, they are still busy." I insisted, "Please! This is an emergency." The operator was not moved. She replied, "Everybody is calling Egypt saying it is an emergency. There was an incident . . ."

"I know! My father was shot! I must speak to my family." The operator was silent for a moment and then said, "Please hold on. I will try my best." She tried for the next forty minutes without luck. Finally, she suggested that I call a special line to the Egyptian embassy in Washington. Within moments, I was talking to the Egyptian ambassador. He tried to reassure me. "Do not worry. Your father is having a minor operation to remove a bullet from his arm."

"How do you know?"

"The minister of defense has informed me from his office. Everything will be fine. In fact, in a little while, you can see me explain on TV what happened." I turned on the TV and switched from channel to channel. My mind was uneasy. Was I getting the truth about my father's condition? Eventually the Egyptian ambassador appeared on the screen and reported that President Sadat was resting comfortably. Hearing him say that on the air was comforting. Yet that did not calm me. Who could relax knowing that their father had been shot? I turned the dial. Now Dan Rather was before me, speaking to the CBS correspondent in Egypt. "What is the latest, Scotty?" His colleague replied, "I just received word . . ." The rest of the sentence was an indistinct mumble.

"I do not hear you well," Rather said, his face showing a strain to comprehend. "Would you repeat what you said?"

"Sadat has passed away," said the voice from halfway around the world.

"Are you sure?"

"Yes, I heard the news from two sources. Mrs. Sadat has left the hospital."

"Thank you, Scotty." Rather looked grimly into the camera. It was as though he were talking to me personally. "We cannot confirm this latest report. Nothing has been announced at the White House yet." A commercial came on, and I sat on the couch across from the TV set, a numbness creeping up my body.

Where were his bodyguards? I asked myself—those huge men who were supposed to throw themselves between my father and any danger? What were they doing with the stun guns they had been given, weapons that could hurl a spark of electricity that would virtually paralyze an attacker fifteen feet or more away? Later, I would hear that Father's bodyguards had been distracted by an air-force jet precision flying team at the moment of the attack. I wondered whether the bodyguards themselves might have been the assassins since at the moment no one knew who had shot my father. Later, India's Indira Gandhi was to lose her life to a personal guard turned assassin.

Everything seemed unreal. The telecast was jumbled, and the English phrase "passed away" somehow sounded so innocuous. I told myself that maybe it was an American idiom that had another meaning. After all, no one had come right out and said, "Sadat is dead."

Half an hour later, at 10:30 A.M., U.S. Senator Howard Baker said it was official. The information had come from the American embassy in Egypt: President Sadat—my father, my president—was dead. My mind recorded the news of his death but I did not absorb it. I could not. I had things to take care of.

Composing myself, I called Lulee's adviser at Brookline High School. There, too, there was confusion because of the news. She did not know of our true identity, but expressed sympathy about what had happened to "your president." She said Lulee was sure to become upset and offered to drive her to our apartment.

As soon as Lulee walked in I knew she had not found out that there had been an assassination. She became aware of the drone of the TV in the background. There we saw a film clip of my father, and U.S. Vice-President Bush appeared and said something about "the terrible loss." Dan Rather appeared again and made it painfully unequivocal. "Now that the vice-president has confirmed the news, we can say with certainty that Anwar Sadat has died."

Lulee started to scream. I hugged her. "It was God's will," I said. It was something I had heard my father and mother, firm in their religious beliefs, say countless times. The Koran, in fact, speaks about the inevitability of death:

> Wherever ye are
> Death will find you out
> Even if you are in towers
> Built up strong and high.

"But, Mommy, Grandfather was right. We never saw him again. We never should have left!" Lulee's words reminded me of my last meeting with my father and his words, "This might be the last time that you see me alive." At this moment, I realized I would not see him again or feel the touch of his hand. We would never be together again in this lifetime.

I tried again to call home and finally got a line. But there was no answer. As soon as I put the receiver down the phone started ringing. For the next hour the calls were almost nonstop. The president's office of the university was calling to say that campus security people were on their way to my apartment. They would help me deal with "the others."

At 12:15 P.M. I opened the door to two university guards whom I had never seen before; they made themselves at home in my living room. My door buzzer rang again. Since the apartment control to trigger the security lock at the street level was unhooked it meant another descent to open the door. The guards went down with me. Two other men said they were looking for Camelia Sadat. The guards asked for their I.D., and they produced FBI identification cards. Back in my apartment, after a few minutes the buzzer sounded once more, and we repeated the scene. The newest callers were also from the U.S. government—this time the State Department—and they also had come to see Camelia Sadat.

Upstairs, we all sat around looking at one other. It was the most people we ever had upstairs, and we barely knew their names. But somehow they all knew who we were. Until then I had felt anonymous in the States. Now, suddenly, it seemed that I was the best-known secret in town. The situation made me feel very public, very vulnerable, even though the men said they had come to protect me.

"You should stay in Boston and wait for the excitement to die down," one of them advised. "I want to go home," I said, thinking of my mother and how she would need me. I also knew that my whole family would be devastated by the news. "We do not think that would be wise because of the situation in Egypt," came the laconic reply. He explained that the assassin was still unknown. Also, it was not clear whether the assassination was the end of the problem or the beginning move to overthrow the Egyptian government. It was not known how many people had been killed, or where my family could be reached. In short, it was not safe.

Until then my thoughts had been focused on my father's death as a personal tragedy. My mind had excluded reflection on why the assassination had been carried out. The shock was too immense for me to absorb more. Was my family in danger? I wondered. Maybe the killers were part of a plot to radically change the Egypt I knew.

I felt as though my mind was shutting down to protect itself. I wanted very much to talk to members of my family in Cairo, and I called out to Farida, our nanny, "Where is the phone?" "You are standing right beside it," Farida said calmly.

I tried to call home again to get firsthand news, but still there was no answer. I called my aunt in Washington and my stepbrother, Gamal, who was in California, and learned that they were to fly home on a private plane arranged by the Egyptian ambassador. Meanwhile, I endured my grief alone while strangers watched. My father was dead, my family was out of touch, and my only contact was with six people who kept telling me to keep my door locked against attackers. They studied me as if I were a delicate piece of china. I felt ready to fall apart.

If I could not be with my family in this tragic time, I thought, I would rather be utterly alone. An Egyptian friend who arrived could not find words of condolence, so he took my hands and held them in his. Strange, I thought, but it is as though my hands do not belong to my body. I cannot feel the warmth of his body, or even the pressure of his grip.

Finally, by 3:30 P.M. everyone was gone. I looked at Lulee, and she fell into my arms. Exhausted and emotionally drained, we remained in that position for a long time. For the next couple of hours Lulee and I sat in front of the TV and hardly moved. It was very strange. They were showing films of my father's life. He was smiling at a crowd, hugging a statesman, proclaiming a victory—always bigger than life, as though he were still there with us, as if he wanted us to know that he was content, that he lived on.

Then the TV began showing pictures of the actual assassination. The murderers were part of the procession. A vehicle stopped unexpectedly. Uniformed men sprang out, weapons in hand. Rifles. Automatic weapons. Repeatedly they sprayed the reviewing stand with bullets. Then some ran up to lob hand grenades into the reviewing stand. In forty-five seconds, it was all over.

They kept talking about him as a "man of peace," and I thought how ironic it was that he was shot while commemorating a war. Yet it was because he made peace with Israel, based on Egypt's strength in that war, that many had wanted to take his life. Then they showed Jihan. In a TV film clip I saw her walking briskly past a gaggle of reporters, her head held high. I saw her controlled gaze. She has great internal strength, I thought. But I still could not help wondering how she was enduring the terrible stress.

As I flipped channels, I saw various versions of the assassination. Satellite communication from half a world away made it possible for television to torture me with the American version, the French version, and the Italian version of the fanatics' assassination of my father. How many times can a man die through the miracle of television? I wondered. As time passed, the ugly event would be repeated again and again.

I wondered whether my father suffered or had died quickly. With every repetition of the film clip depicting the attack I felt as if my own body were being ripped by the bullets. Why did the bodyguards not jump to shield Father's body? I would later learn that Father's secretary, Fawzi Abdel Hafez, threw his own body on top of Father's, trying in vain to save him. Fawzi, who had handled all Father's private matters, first became his personal bodyguard in 1956. He served his master with the tenacity and utter devotion of a fierce bulldog. His stubbornness in protecting my father's interests had angered many people over the years. When the bullets were fired, he instinctively threw himself in front of Father, absorbing more than twenty bullets. Incredibly, he lived. He stayed a year in the Navy hospital in Washington, although after many operations he still carries a bullet in his lung and is crippled for life.

I remember the PLO leader Yasir Arafat being photographed flashing a hand sign that meant victory. And Libya's Qaddafi seemed to be trying to claim credit for the assassination. It is ironic, I thought, that some Arabs are so eager to celebrate Father's death, while another TV clip showed Israel's Menachem Begin, a long-term enemy and a hard-line adversary even at Camp David, nearly in tears over the realization that Father had been murdered. I never in my life thought about killing anyone, but that night I could have murdered my father's assassins.

There were brief episodes on the TV that gave me respite. Some programs showed Father talking, laughing, and joking with officials and with interviewers. For moments at a time it almost became possible to forget that he was dead.

The sun was sinking, and the light in the room was growing softer. Lulee stood up. She announced that we had to eat. I will never forget how she took charge that night. She took me to the kitchen, cooked soup, and insisted that I eat. When I told her that I could not, she maneuvered me to the dining table and fed me as though I were a baby. I do not remember saying a word at the table. I just remember Lulee holding my hands while, in the living room, the voice on the TV continued to praise my father. It gave us something to cling to.

Lulee led me back to the couch after dinner and continued to mother me. She kissed me and told me I should let myself cry. I could not. Our religion says we should not shed more than one tear for a loved one, lest we disturb the spirit of the departed, but I could not even muster that one tear.

At 11:00 P.M., the late news recapped the day's nightmare. I was transfixed as the new Egyptian president, Husni Mubarak, announced the death of my father to the Egyptian people. The new president, I said to myself. It did not seem real. Mubarak spoke of continuing Sadat's course toward peace. I wondered if he could do it. I wondered if my father's spirit would rest easy.

The phone rang for the last time that day. It was the instructor of my writing class, Nancy Finn. "Camelia," she said, "I just want you to know that I think your president was a great man." I heard Lulee click off our TV. I felt a chill. There was a moment of silence before the caller continued, "All I can say is that I am very sorry. As a Jew and a fellow human being, my heart feels sick. What they did is tragic—for all of us."

"Yes, they killed him," I said as tears seared my eyes and spilled down my cheeks. "They killed my father."

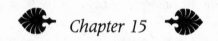

Chapter 15

THE FORTY–DAY CEREMONY IN EGYPT

THE DAY AFTER THE ASSASSINATION, I telephoned my mother's home in Cairo. It was the first time I was able to get through to Cairo. Until now, no one from the family had reached me in Boston—not even the Egyptian ambassador or any other member of the government.

I felt nervous as I waited, not knowing how to begin the conversation. If whoever answered the phone reacted emotionally, I worried that I would break down. It was my mother. From what I could hear, she and my sisters were in emotional turmoil. It was 1:00 P.M. in Boston and 7:00 P.M. in Cairo. Both Mother and I were frantic and began crying. Mother passed the phone to Rawia, who in turn began crying. Then my mother took the phone again. She controlled her sobbing, and spoke. "Why did you not come on the plane that the ambassador arranged for your brother, Gamal?"

"I knew nothing about that plane," I said. "No one called me at all." It was incredible, perhaps, but true.

"I am coming on a plane that will get there before the funeral," I told my mother. I had learned via TV that Husni Mubarak, who was acting head of state, had announced that a national funeral for my father would be held that Saturday.

Then I heard Rawia's voice on the phone, "Even your stepmother, Jihan, says you should not come." That confirmed what the officers in Boston had advised.

"I have also been moved from my apartment because of security concerns," I said.

·

Two days later the Egyptian ambassador called from Washington. It was the first time he had spoken to me since he assured me that my father had only been wounded on October 6. He did not say anything about the plane to Cairo or why he had not invited me to go along. "Your brother, Gamal, called from Egypt and asked if you spoke to the U.S. press against Husni Mubarak, saying that he killed your father."

"No! How can you ask such a thing? As ambassador you must follow the press or at least review clippings. Have you seen such a thing?"

"No. I told your brother that I had not seen anything like that, and defended you. I just wanted to check with you." He continued, "It seems someone told President Mubarak that you had made a statement. He conferred with Gamal, and Gamal contacted me."

The ambassador's voice turned solicitous, as though he were talking friend to friend. "I think that after the election you should send a congratulatory telegram to Mr. Mubarak. That should take care of the matter." Then he advised me about what the proposed telegram should say. As I thought about this, I was furious. I could not figure out who would initiate such a rumor at a time of extreme grief for my family. The anti-Sadat gossips were already trying to create problems for the family and smear Father's memory. This would be only the beginning, I suspected.

Two days later Abdallah Abdelbary, the editor of *Al-Ahram*, the major Cairo newspaper for which I had been writing articles, called from Egypt.

"You plan to come back to Cairo?"

"No."

"I think you should return," he said.

"Why?"

"I do not need a correspondent there."

I did not need news like that at this time. Furthermore, Abdallah Abdelbary was family. He is my daughter's uncle. I suspected that Abdallah was sensitive to changes in power, and the Sadats were thrust into the role of political outsiders the moment my father died.

My patience snapped. "I did not come to Boston to work as a correspondent," I said. "I came to get an education." In my time, I had overcome worse obstacles than the one he was putting before me. I knew I could do it again, somehow.

•

I continued to attend Boston University classes until the forty-day commemoration of my father's death, when I planned to return to Egypt. Some of my classmates thought it interesting that I dressed in black, especially two friends from the Philippines who knew me as Camelia Mohammed. "It is strange that you care for him so much," said one of them when I explained that I was mourning President Sadat. My Liberian classmate, Lamini, also talked with me at some length. I felt like crying, but, this time, true to my religion, I restrained my tears.

I had tried three times to reach Jihan in Cairo by phone. I talked with her secretary. "She is busy," the secretary said. I wondered: Doing what? At Egyptian funerals ladies sit and do nothing. I had called my stepmother to offer condolences. I was calling from across the ocean—and she was too busy to give me her ear, even for a few moments. That frustrated and hurt me.

I called Rokaya. "Tell our stepmother that I do not need anything from her. I had to call her three times and she is too busy to talk to me."

·

My mother was more upset by Father's death than I could have imagined—even more than she had been at the death of her own mother. Divorce had not lessened Mother's love for my father. Our religion requires that those bereaved in the family of the one who has died should recite the words of the holy Koran so that the words will reach and comfort the soul of the departed. In her mind my mother believed this, but she became crazy with grief when she heard the news.

At the sound of her anguished cries people from all thirty-two flats in the building came to look in on her. "He loved them so much!" she sobbed. "He called them 'my children.' And they betrayed him. They betrayed him!"

·

Rokaya had become hysterical at the time of the assassination. She had been watching the military parade on TV; she heard the bullets. The TV coverage was cut as the shooting began. Rawia had been in her kitchen at the time of the assassination. One of her sons, who had been watching the parade on TV, called out that the coverage had been interrupted. "I think there was shooting," he told his mother.

Rawia called Rokaya, who lived about ten miles away. "I am going to Mother's," she said. En route, she was stopped at a police cordon. She explained that she was Sadat's daughter and was trying to get home to find out what had happened. The police allowed her to pass. Rokaya did not show up at our mother's house. Rawia called. A maid said Rokaya had gone to President Sadat's home. Rawia left to join her. They were turned away from Father's home and turned back by roadblocks when they tried to reach the hospital. Finally they went to the office of the presidential secretary, near Father's home, where they were assured that he had only been wounded. They were advised to go home. Rokaya refused to leave.

They did not know it, but Jihan and her children, and grandson, who had been at the parade, arrived at Father's home by helicopter. Jihan then left for the hospital. As a result of Jihan's stopover, the presidential secretary learned about the shooting. It was not known then that our father was dead. It was only said that Father's personal secretary, Fawzi Abdel Hafez, died trying to protect the president with his body. It turned out to be an erroneous report.

Rawia left Rokaya at the office of the presidential secretary and went to our mother's house. Rokaya eventually got to Father's home. At about 3:30 P.M., Rokaya's maid called Mother's home with the terrible news. "I am sorry. President Sadat has died." Mother and Rawia got the news from a maid.

•

In Mit Abul-Kum, the villagers became hysterical when they heard the news. People wept loudly, tearing at their clothes and beating their faces. Many simply started running toward Cairo and later got on buses to the city. At Anwar el-Sadat's funeral the people of Mit Abul-Kum were well represented, along with the world's leaders. In the meantime, people from neighboring villages came to Mit Abul-Kum to offer their condolences to the village for the loss of its son.

•

Here in the United States, between the assassination and the funeral there were four days of almost continual reporting and discussion about the death of Anwar el-Sadat, his life, and the implications of the assassination. I doubt whether Egypt itself had even one percent of the media coverage the United States provided.

I saw interviews of my father by Walter Cronkite, Barbara Walters, and others that never appeared in Egypt because they were in

English. As I watched my father's animated face, living again on the color TV screen, I could not believe he was dead. I did not want to believe it. Then I was struck with a hopeful thought. Would it not be like him to announce his own death, just to see what worldwide reaction would be? I recalled that in 1973, he engaged in a bit of fakery to put the enemy off-balance prior to the October War. He announced that one military leader had to leave Egypt for a cancer treatment. He had other information leaked indicating that other leaders who were critical to a war effort had gone away on trips. If he had used false information once, I mused, he might be capable of faking his own death. Then I realized all that was wishful thinking.

As I followed events in the media it was brought home to me that my father had indeed gained the status of an international statesman. I was here in the States when the Soviet head of state, Brezhnev, died. He was the head of a world superpower, but the United States press gave relatively little attention to his death as compared with the detailed discussion given my father.

Through television, he had become a virtual member of households throughout the United States and the world. His earnestness and simplicity became evident. He was seen as a symbol of hope and peace. Time after time these beliefs have been echoed as individuals have talked with me about their feelings for my father. I was surprised that in Boston, even synagogues held group prayers for my father's soul.

I was also tremendously impressed by the fact that three former U.S. presidents—Carter, Nixon, and Ford—attended the funeral of this Arab head of state. I do not know whether any other Arab statesman has been accorded such an honor by a world superpower, or ever will be again. Various other leaders and dignitaries also attended Father's military funeral. I remember seeing Schmidt of Germany, Giscard d'Estaing of France, Britain's Prince Charles, Nimeiry of the Sudan, Alexander Haig from the United States, and numerous others. Actually, it is rare that any fallen head of state anywhere in the world is accorded such a distinction.

I feel tremendously moved to know that so many people's hearts and minds were touched by my father's vision and his willingness to make the highest sacrifice for the principles he held most dear.

•

The time came for me to go back to Egypt for the forty-day commemoration of my father's death. At the airport in Cairo, my mother was waiting in a VIP car. But initially I walked right past her, not recognizing the grief-stricken woman who had come to meet me. She looked shorter and much thinner and her face was anguished.

I began to weep. I do not know whether it was because it hurt me to see her looking like this, or because I was now in the city where my father had been assassinated, or just that the strain and mixed feelings associated with my return were too much to bear. As I began to weep my mother spoke sharply to me. "Stop it! We are in public!" At the graveside ceremony, people would nudge me when I began to cry, "Oh! My father . . ." When I turned my attention from my mother I saw that Rawia and her sons were there, as were many friends and colleagues. We later went to my mother's home to await the forty-day ceremony, which started the next day.

During the ceremony we saw the other members of the family. Jihan and her daughters Noha and Lobna were in control of themselves, as was Rawia. Rokaya, our stepsister Jihan, and I sobbed. Nana (young Jihan) had been especially hard hit by our father's death. Normally, she was frail, but now she appeared to weigh only sixty pounds or so. She had enjoyed a very close bond with Father and had spent much time with him in recent years. After the forty-day ceremony, we went to Father's home to visit Jihan and her children.

.

During my first days in Cairo, my mind continued to dwell on the rumor that was designed to be a wedge between me and President Mubarak—that I had given a U.S. press interview that was hostile to him. I wanted to get that straightened out. It could not do any good for relationships between President Mubarak and me or my family if it were left unchallenged. Also, I suspected it had something to do with my being discharged as a correspondent for *Al-Ahram*. I talked to Rawia and told her about the talk with Abdallah Abdelbary. I said I wanted to talk with President Mubarak about the rumor.

President Mubarak had called Gamal, my stepbrother, to meet with him. If Jihan or any of her family or any of Sadat's first family wanted anything, the president said, they were to communicate it to him through Gamal. Similarly, if Mubarak had anything to say to the members of Sadat's families, he would convey it through Gamal.

Husni Mubarak was somewhat apart from the Sadat clan, whereas many of Father's colleagues whom he had known since the revolution were viewed, at least in the households of my mother and sisters, as members of the family. Mubarak was younger, and when he was the air force chief, Father began to promote a political career for him. To the best of my knowledge, the relationship was more professional than personal.

I called Father's house and asked to see Gamal. As in the past, we were not allowed to just drop in. After a couple of days, Gamal called me to arrange a meeting.

On the appointed day, I went to Father's home. Upon entering, I found Jihan entertaining some ladies in her reception room. There were two reception rooms, one for Jihan and another larger one for my father. I went on to Father's reception room, where Gamal was waiting.

Gamal was kind, but reserved, as usual. His profession of chemical engineer matches his personality—serious and quiet-spoken. I told him about my experience with Abdallah Abdelbary. "Would you please tell Mr. Mubarak about this and see if you can explain what happened? I really would like to settle matters and see if I can get my job with *Al-Ahram* back." I was not supported by any scholarship. The correspondent's job had been the key to my being able to survive while studying for my master's degree.

"Abdallah was calling me daily after Father's death," Gamal said. "He was asking, 'Why is Camelia staying in Boston? Why does she not come back?' and saying, 'I do not need her there.' I told him, 'Camelia does what she wants.' I also said that if she stays we can support her."

Gamal said that Mubarak had called him to ask about the press interview. It was clear that Gamal had not subscribed to the rumor—unlike Father, who often seemed to believe the worst if it in any way touched on his reputation. "I called our ambassador to Washington because I wanted to check whether I was correct," Gamal said. That was something Father would not have done. I still do not know, though, whether President Mubarak ever was told that the rumor was unfounded.

"I am not going to talk further with Husni Mubarak about this," said Gamal. "I will try to find a solution to help you. Before Father died, he asked me to take care of my elder sisters Rokaya, Rawia, and Camelia, just as I would my own sisters, Lobna, Noha, and Jihan. He said he wanted me to give special attention to you and Rawia, since he felt life had been difficult for you. Just rely on me," he said, looking at me sincerely. "Leave it to me."

Two days later, I got a call from Gamal. He wanted to see me. When I arrived at Father's house, I was led to the terrace, where Gamal and his wife were sitting, along with Jihan and her children. Everyone greeted me warmly. Gamal told me he wanted me to go with him to Father's room. There, he said, "I will arrange for payments to you equal to what *Al-Ahram* was paying until you complete your graduate program in Boston."

I was happy at the display of family solidarity. Perhaps the lines that began to be drawn between the children of the two Sadat families after Father became president might be blurred or erased after his death, I thought. It would be good for both sides.

"I really do not think I can accept," I said. "You are my brother— but how can I accept?" The offer was generous, but what Gamal was offering represented a substantial burden for him, I knew.

Gamal was insistent. "You are my sister. You know what my father asked me to do. We are all supportive."

The statement was simple and straightforward, and it touched me deeply.

"God willing, I will be able to complete my degree," I said. "But then, I want you to consider this as a loan that I intend to repay."

Gamal gave me a kiss. He kept his word. He was to send me money regularly till my graduation from Boston University.

Our shared grief over Father's death has done much to bring the two halves of Father's family together, which is something he would have wanted.

•

Our family expressed their grief in different ways. Rokaya, who had never cried, would watch the assassination over and over again on video, while the tears streamed from her eyes and she wept herself to the point of stupor.

Rawia, who as a child would cry over the death of a butterfly, and had remained sensitive to the slightest hurts, was shocked to the core. Dry-eyed, she continued her life with seeming indifference. Two years later, she visited me in Boston and spent most of her time visiting hospitals for diagnosis of her growing number of ailments. In the end, she was told that most of them were a result of her locked-in grief and she has had to learn to cry again.

The way my father died has never left my mother's mind, and she talks of it with vivid recollection. She has been plagued, too, by the many problems of age that she confronts without the will to live. Only recently she survived a near-fatal coma, and I am constantly fearful for her. I remember her in her apartment surrounded by the pictures of Father that have filled it since my earliest recollection. She has told me of her treasures—the letters that Father wrote to her while he was in jail and the photographs taken during his child-hood. When she dies, she says, she wants these precious mementoes to be given to Gamal, my father's only son, whom she has always considered her adopted son.

The only thing that sustains her is the annual celebration of my father's birthday in Mit Abul-Kum. It was a tradition my father established and the village welcomed the chance to honor its fa-vored son. I think of her now returning to her village every De-cember 25 to cook lamb and other dishes for the poor people of the village, who otherwise never see such abundance. And I'm sure that sometimes she must smell the sweet, strong fragrance of jasmine and remember the young Ekbal and her handsome soldier suitor courting through the open window of her mother's house.

Envoi

On a windy day I returned to Nasser City outside Cairo to visit Father's grave by myself. The site is lonely, desolate. It is part of what was once a military zone. Apart from a 120,000-seat soccer stadium, which is some distance away, no major buildings mark the area. Nearby stands the tomb of Egypt's unknown soldier, erected in 1976.

A narrow military road once cut through the area. The government widened it after the 1973 October War with Israel to form a parade ground for military celebrations. It contains a stonework reviewing stand with marble floors. It was in this reviewing stand that Father sat along with Vice-President Husni Mubarak, the minister of defense, and others on October 6, 1981, to view a military procession held in remembrance of the Egyptian victory in the October War. The assassins struck during that parade.

I walked around, looking at the monument to my father. I read his epitaph again and again. It contains a sura from the Koran, followed by the words Father wrote for his own grave before he made his trip to Jerusalem.

> Think not of those
> Who are slain in Allah's way
> As dead. Nay, they live
> Finding their sustenance
> In the presence of their Lord.
>
> President Mohammed Anwar el-Sadat.
> Hero of War—Hero of Peace
> Lived for Peace and Martyred for His Principles.
> 1918–1981.

I thought it was ironic that Father, who loved people so much, had been laid to rest in such an isolated place. His will was to be buried in his beloved Mit Abul-Kum, along with his parents and his stepbrother 'Atif. But the government decided on this site because it would be more accessible to visitors.

In the distance I could see the reviewing stand across the boulevard. It is a sort of monument in itself. The stones that make up the stand are still marred by the many bullets that struck on October 6. The reviewing stand has not been used by President Mubarak since the day of the assassination.

As I looked across at the reviewing stand I felt I could hear the crack of rifles and the chattering of machine guns. I had hated the thought of his body ripped to ribbons by machine guns. It was not until my return to Cairo that I learned that there had only been three wounds: one in the knee, another in his arm, and the fatal one, which had entered his chest on his left side. I had seen the new blue military uniform he had been wearing when he was killed. It seems small, much too small for my father, I thought illogically. I had glimpsed his human frailty and it scared me.

In his sixty-one years on this earth, Father had risen from humble surroundings in Mit Abul-Kum to become a world leader. It took forty-five seconds to end his life. Forty-five seconds to kill a man who had the courage to attempt to lead Egypt, Israel, and the Middle East out of a centuries-old jungle of religious and political hatred. Forty-five seconds for fanatics to take away the father whom I had spent most of my thirty-two years on this earth pursuing, but whom I never felt confident I had touched with my love.

I looked at the slab above my father's tomb again. I wondered if it were true, as my mother so fervently believed, that the spirit of my father still lingered somewhere nearby. So close, even, that he could hear me. "Send up your prayers to your father," she had told me many times. "Read from the holy Koran to comfort him." Even when she visited Lulee and me in Boston the next year, in June 1982, she continued to implore that I continue my prayers for my father. Our belief is that the soul of the departed stays near his loved ones, and I knew that despite all of our differences, my father did love me greatly.

I wish I could send my thoughts to you, Father, I thought as I stood there on the windy strip. More than anything in this world, I would like you to hear me now. I wish, too, that I could hear your voice, see your face, and touch you once again. I still need your help and your wisdom, Father. It seems more like decades than months since we parted, and now I know I must face the rest of my life without being able to see you.

The desert wind tugged at my hair and clothing. The dryness of the wind felt cool on my skin. Tears filled my eyes. Suddenly I felt more alone than I had ever felt before, and screams that seemed to come from a long way tore from my opened mouth. The enormity of my loss struck with full force and I, a grown woman, was as lost and terrified as a child in a nightmare.

Incongruous details spilled into my mind. I remembered how you had always liked my hair to be long and would touch it appreciatively. How gentle and caring you were to my mother. How I loved to hear you talk deeply and softly to me, pulling at your pipe as you stared meditatively into the distance, at a place known only to you. Perhaps you saw the muddy river of your boyhood, the glorious Nile that links us to an ancient heritage. Perhaps you saw the young boy who had not been able to swim and who had listened enchanted to the stories his grandmother told him. I thought of how I would never see your familiar and beautiful face smile with un-looked-for pleasure at some joke I made. And then with a quick, stabbing pain that made me scream once more, I remembered, absurdly, the hurt I had caused you when for a while I stopped kissing your hand. I saw your face darken with unspoken anger, your jaw working impatiently. I had done it out of childish petulance, to punish you for hurting me, but now I realized that this would be the thing that would always haunt me. The thing I could never undo, or remedy with fresh tenderness and kisses. And I shall bear this memory, unatoned, with me for the rest of my life.

I was exhausted, but my voice continued to sound in my head. I felt as though I were listening to myself, my lips still as thoughts spoke themselves. I wanted so much to tell you of my love, Father, during our last three years together, but I thought you would judge me weak.

I loved you more than you could ever know. I wish we could go to Mit Abul-Kum as we did when I was a child a thousand more times. You gave me a love and reverence for the people and the traditions of our land that I shall always remember. Perhaps I should have spent my life in the village, accepting an age-old role. But I was caught up in the changes our country went through, which, to many people, you yourself represented. In this new world I have tried to find a place for myself and the old ways you taught me. And if I can give my daughter a small part of what you gave me, she will be richer than kings.

There was a time when I was bitter—unhappy about the things you did to me, and the things you did not do. It is all in this book, the letter I never wrote you. Now I am no longer bitter. My mother also taught me well. I remember being hurt that you would not hear of my troubles. But Mother held my arm tight and implored me to forgive you. For only God has the right to judge, and we can only clear our hearts and forgive utterly what is not ours to judge.

You said to me once in Mit Abul-Kum that you would not leave us an inheritance of money, but that we would inherit a wealth of love and pride, and that it was our duty to invest that inheritance for our grandchildren. Now, in my life in the United States, I am received with love and kindness because of you, and I can understand more deeply what you meant that day and hope that I can use wisely the legacy you gave me.

Your life was shaped long before I was born. And now it will be shaped by history. World leaders have called you great; historians are calling you a man of courage and wisdom. Your story, like that of your hero Zahran, may yet be told to some impressionable child who yearns for tales of courage and sacrifice far beyond the village horizons.

I am not a world leader, a historian, or a maker of ballads. And in these pages I have only tried to tell the story of a daughter's love for her father.

Index